Vaccinat[illegible]es or No?

Helping You Decide

(UK edition)

Will Sussman MA
Lara Sussman MSc

First published by The Merrydown Publishing Company Ltd in 2003

ISBN 0 9545106 0 7

Printed by: The Waverley Press, Ryde, Isle of Wight PO33 2QD

Cover Design: Liz Vinycomb

Every care has been taken when writing this book, to ensure the accuracy of the material provided. However the authors cannot accept responsibility for any damage or harm caused by any advice or information given in this book. If you have any doubts about vaccinations, you should consult a medically qualified practitioner.

The Merrydown Publishing Company Ltd
PO Box 89
Seaview
Isle of Wight
PO34 5ZQ

www.vaccinations-yesorno.co.uk

Tel: 08707 2000 67

CONTENTS

Author's Note

When we first started looking into whether or not to vaccinate our children, we very quickly found that much of the information was biased. Our doctor insisted that vaccines were 100% safe, whilst the anti-vaccination lobby vigorously campaigned against childhood jabs. We discovered that both camps had often used the same piece of medical research to further their own arguments, and that scientific results had not always been presented fairly. We felt that there must be a middle ground, where common sense rather than propaganda, prevailed. In this book we present the facts, as we know them, to help you decide what to do.

Lara completed pre-clinical medicine before having our first child. She is now training to be a homoeopath, and has an MSc in child development. Will was a radio producer at Classic FM for 10 years and is now a writer. We have two children and are continually debating the vaccination issues.

For Annie and Freddie - long may you stay healthy.

INTRODUCTION

To vaccinate or not to vaccinate?

In the last few years, we have been bombarded with so many different opinions and facts about vaccination, that most of us must be utterly confused. Read one newspaper article and you'll go straight down to your surgery to vaccinate your child. Turn on the TV the same day and you'll fear for your child if he ever came near a doctor's needle.

Many of the diseases that we are protecting our children against are deadly, some are very serious but not fatal, and others are unpleasant but rarely have serious side effects. The vaccination programme has clearly been a factor in the reduction of the number of cases of childhood disease, but we, as parents, are now asking at what price has this been achieved.

Everyday we read conclusive arguments from both camps - those for and those against vaccinations. Everyday we hear stories of children who allegedly suffer from autism as a result of the MMR jab. At the same time, we read stories of another measles outbreak in some part of the country. What we very rarely see is a breakdown of the number of people that have suffered as a result of a vaccine, or of the number of people who suffer serious illness or death by contracting one of the diseases. If we had these figures in front of us, we would see that there is truth in both arguments, but more importantly it would help us, the parents, to weigh up the risks, and then decide whether to vaccinate our children or not. It is not as easy as that, of course. There is more to the argument than just numbers. We need to know how effective the vaccines are, what are the supposed side effects, what indeed are the diseases themselves that we are trying to protect against, and how deadly are they.

In this book, we have tried to take a measured view, and present the facts, as we know them, from both sides of the fence. We will show figures listing the incidence of the disease in Britain. We will also consider the likelihood of your child suffering from side effects of the vaccinations.

There are alternatives to conventional immunisation, when dealing with childhood disease. None will protect against getting the disease itself, but they may lessen the severity of the disease. For example, some homoeopaths will administer "nosodes" to a child instead of the conventional vaccination. These nosodes strengthen the areas of the body that the particular disease would affect. If your child did then contract the disease, it should be in a milder form. Homoeopathic remedies administered during an illness, can also lead to a less severe case of that disease. And if you did vaccinate your child, homoeopathy can be used to protect him against the side effects of the vaccination. See Appendix 2 for more information on homoeopathy.

Table 1: Timetable of Childhood Immunisations [1]

When to immunise	**What is given**	**How it is given**
2, 3 & 4 months old	Polio Diphtheria, tetanus, pertussis and Hib (DTP-Hib) Meningitis C	By mouth One injection One injection
Around 13 months old	Measles, mumps and rubella (MMR)	One injection
3 to 5 years old	Polio Diphtheria, tetanus and acellular pertussis (DTaP) Measles, mumps and rubella (MMR)	By mouth One injection One injection
10 to 14 years old (and sometimes shortly after birth)	BCG (against tuberculosis)	Skin test, then if needed, one injection
13 to 18 years old	Diphtheria and tetanus (Td) Polio	One injection By Mouth

By the time your child is four months old, if you follow the immunisation programme, he will have had 18 vaccines (see Table 1, above), and then he'll have the MMR triple jab at 13 months. Many regard this as a fantastic achievement towards banishing childhood disease. Others feel that we are overloading our children with harmful substances, and helping to reduce their immune system. The good news in the UK is that we still have a choice as to whether to vaccinate or not. Most schools don't insist on vaccination prior to enrolment, and most doctors won't wipe you off their books if you don't have the jabs.

This book will give you the information to make that choice. You may go whole-heartedly for vaccinations; you may decide to vaccinate but to wait till your baby is older and stronger; or you may take a piecemeal approach - choosing to vaccinate against some illnesses and not others. You may want to try an alternative approach to vaccination; or to use homoeopathy in conjunction with vaccination; or you may want to avoid vaccinations altogether. Luckily, the choice is still yours - good luck in making it.

Finally, despite all the hype and bad press we read, it is worth remembering that the numbers involved are small. Very few people suffer serious reactions to vaccinations, and these days, very few people, in the UK, are left seriously ill or dead following a childhood disease.

---

1 A new guide to childhood immunisations, Health Promotion England, and the NHS. 2001.

CHAPTER 1

THE TWO SIDES OF THE DEBATE

Why doctors recommend vaccinations:

- Many doctors believe that vaccinations are one of medical science's greatest success stories, responsible for wiping out many deadly infectious diseases.

- Many of the vaccinations protect against diseases for which there may not be a cure.[1]

- If there is a cure for the disease, surely prevention is better than cure.

- Bacteria that cause disease are developing resistance to the antibiotic cures. In these cases, vaccines are the only reliable tools to prevent disease. [2]

- The theory states that if enough people get vaccinated, the disease will disappear. Smallpox is an example of a disease successfully wiped out using immunisation. In order to eliminate a disease the vaccination levels have to run at 95%. This means that 95 in every 100 children have to be vaccinated for the disease to be effectively wiped out. This is known as herd protection, and doctors hope that other diseases such as measles and mumps can soon be banished.

- "Vaccination is the single most cost-effective health intervention." [3]

- Some doctors believe that vaccinations strengthen the immune system.

- The WHO believes that immunisation is "a key element of public health…a crucial element in enabling every child to reach his/her full physical and intellectual potential." [4]

- We are in a cycle. When a disease is prevalent, everybody wants a vaccine to control the disease. With the success of the vaccine, the disease becomes rare, and so people pay more attention to the side-effects of the vaccine. Fewer children are immunised, and as a result the incidence of disease increases. This cycle has been going on ever since the introduction of vaccinations, so the latest rumblings by parents and media are nothing new. We should continue with the vaccination programme undaunted.

- Doctors believe that in many cases vaccines are wrongly blamed for side effects. Often, developmental abnormalities, like fits, seizures and autism, first appear in the early years of life, just at a time when the immunisation programme is taking place.[5]

- As with all medicines, some people will experience serious side effects. But the number of people that do suffer a serious reaction is so small, that it does not outweigh the good that vaccinations bring.

- The government pays GP surgeries for each child immunised. There is a financial bonus for reaching vaccination targets, and missing these targets would put financial pressure on the surgery.[6]

Why homoeopaths suggest an alternative to vaccination:

- Homoeopaths believe that the death rate from infectious childhood diseases has declined due to better sanitation, hygiene and nutrition levels, and improved housing, and not just because of the immunisation programmes.

- Homoeopaths point out, that even if you do accept that vaccination programmes have been responsible for the reduction in disease, epidemics still occur. For example, 18 years after the compulsory smallpox vaccination was introduced, England experienced its worst smallpox epidemic of the nineteenth century, when 44,000 people died.[7] Unless vaccines are 100% effective, and unless all children are vaccinated (two unlikely scenarios), mass immunisation will never completely eradicate the disease.[8]

- Alternative practitioners believe that the virus or bacteria is never truly wiped out but can alter itself into a different, related, disease. They believe that by trying to eliminate often harmless diseases like mumps we are creating a situation where new, and maybe more serious, diseases will appear. Dr Vera Scheibner has reported a 399% increase in the incidence of disease caused by infection of the Hib bacteria since the 1940s. She asks "Why have developed countries experienced such an increase in invasive infections in the last forty years? The best demonstrable common factor in this period is a documented push for mass vaccination." [9]

- Homoeopaths are concerned that foreign material is injected directly into our bloodstream, rather than being processed by our body's normal defence systems - namely the skin, mucous membranes and digestive system.

- Homoeopaths believe that vaccinations weaken the immune system. They fear that no-one has investigated the long-term effects of giving an infant at least 18 different jabs by the time he is four months old, and 21 vaccinations by the time he is 15 months old. They wonder just how many vaccines an immature immune system can handle. There are two reasons why the Government starts jabs in the first year. First, some of the diseases in question are at their most dangerous if caught by infants under the age of one, and second, the Government believes that "starting the programme early and having short intervals, reduces the opportunities for failing to complete a course" [10] of vaccinations.

- Homoeopaths believe that childhood diseases are beneficial to the child. After an illness, a child will often experience a physical and/or mental developmental leap. Furthermore, contracting a childhood disease can help wipe out inherited traits such as asthma and eczema. For example, a study in Guinea-Bissau found that children who had contracted measles naturally, were less likely to suffer from eczema, asthma and/or hay fever than children who had been vaccinated.[11]

- Homoeopaths believe that many of the diseases we are vaccinated against, such as measles or mumps, are not the potential killers we are led to believe. They point out that most people aged over 30 have had measles.

- Research shows that protection afforded by a vaccination is always inferior to that given by natural infection.[12]

- No vaccine is 100% safe.[13]

- Some homoeopaths would argue that vaccines work imperfectly, and at an unacceptable cost to your child's health.

- Homoeopaths believe that if your child has a healthy lifestyle, and eats a good balanced diet, then he is less likely to catch a disease, and if he does, it will affect him less severely.

The pros and cons of multiple jabs

These days many vaccines are administered in one injection. If you follow the government guidelines, your child will have three triple jabs, and three quadruple jabs by the time he is five years old. These polyvalent vaccines, as scientists call them, are a huge benefit to the vaccination programme. A child will gain protection against three or four illnesses from just one visit to his GP. This means that many more children are likely to be immunised, and so herd protection can be attained. It also reduces the huge cost of the vaccination programme.

Many people argue that it is ill-advised to give a child a triple or quadruple jab. We don't know how the individual components of the polyvalent vaccines work together. Their effectiveness could be reduced. And then there is the question of side effects. We are giving our children three or four viruses that they would be very unlikely to catch at the same time naturally. Some scientists ask whether a child's immune system can cope with a triple hit at once.[14]

---

1 Aventis Pasteur MSC website.
2 WHO, Weekly Epidemiological Record, 1998, 73, 64-71.
3 Aventis Pasteur MSC website.
4 Global Alliance for Vaccines and Immunization (GAVI), on the WHO website.
5 Chen & Stefano, The Lancet 1998; 351: 611-12.
6 Heller et al, BMJ 2001; 323: 838-840.
7 Lynne McTaggart. The Vaccination Bible. What Doctors Don't Tell You, 1997.
8 McLean, The Lancet 1995: 345; 272.
9 www.whale.to/v/beattie.html
10 Salisbury & Begg, Immunisation against infectious disease, Dept of Health, HMSO, 1996.
11 Shaheen et al, The Lancet 1996; 347: 1792-6.
12 J H Joncas, Canadian Medical Association Journal, 1983; 129: 110-112.
13 Chen & Stefano, The Lancet, op. cit.
14 Wakefield & Montgomery, Adverse Drug Reaction Toxicol. Rev. 2000; 19: 284 - 292.

CHAPTER 2

THE ISSUE OF SIDE EFFECTS

As we've mentioned in chapter 1, some people will react to vaccinations, just as some people react to a medicine. Some health officials deny that there are any side effects to jabs. They do this because they are worried that people will refuse to have their jabs. Others admit that there are side effects, but that the chances of being seriously damaged by a jab are so small, that it is worth the risk, in order to provide protection against disease. Many alternative practitioners believe that every time your child has a jab you are poisoning him.

What we can say for certain is that some people do react to vaccines. Between 1990 and 1995, 80 million doses of vaccination were given in the UK, and there were 5,433 reports of an adverse reaction to a jab, and most of these were mild. In 1995, when 14 million jabs were given, there were 152 serious reactions. That's about one serious reaction for every 100,000 jabs.[1]

It should be said that many reactions go unreported, or that a connection is not made linking the reaction to the vaccine. Furthermore, official guidelines advise that a reaction must occur within 72 hours of a killed vaccine, and within 14 days of a live vaccine.[2] Any reaction beyond these timescales is not attributed to the vaccine. So, bearing this in mind, it is understandable why other studies have shown higher rates for side effects, with one serious reaction for every 3000 doses of vaccine.[3]

Many studies compare one vaccination against another. Many studies only look at side effects within the first few days of a jab. And many studies are funded by the vaccine manufacturers. Ideally, what we need is more studies that compare vaccinated children with non-vaccinated children, and that take a long term view by monitoring children months or even years after the vaccination programme is completed.

The Government acknowledges that some people will suffer side effects from vaccinations, and has set up a vaccine damage payment scheme to allow for this. Parents can claim up to £100,000[4] if their children have "suffered severe mental and/or physical disablement of 80% or more. . . . It is not compensation, but is designed to ease the present and future burdens." [5]

It is important that you discuss your child's medical history with your doctor before having any jabs. Make sure you tell your doctor if your child or any other family member has reacted to a jab in the past. This is vital information that should be taken into account when considering whether or not to vaccinate.

In each chapter we will discuss the side effects of a jab, and where possible, we'll try and give you an idea of the risks involved. Some reactions are caused by the small amount of disease bacteria in the vaccination. Other reactions are allergic reactions to one or more of the vaccine's ingredients. These are known as anaphylactic reactions. They can be delayed for up to 72 hours after a jab. If your child develops breathlessness, swelling, a rash or unexpected symptoms, you should seek medical attention. If your child suffers a serious anaphylactic shock, he should be taken to hospital and given adrenaline.

Government figures show that between 1992 and 1995, 55 million doses of vaccination were administered, and there were 87 reports of anaphylactic reaction. So for about every 600,000 doses, one child will suffer a very serious allergic reaction.[6]

After your child has a jab, you should monitor him closely for any reaction. If you are at all worried, you should seek medical advice. If your worries are unfounded, and the reaction is not serious, at least your doctor will have been told about a mild side effect to a jab. The more people that report side effects, the better we'll be able to monitor the jabs being given to our children.

Serious side effects are very rare, but you must seek medical advice immediately if your child has any of these reactions following a jab: [7]

- A fever of 38.5ºC or over
- Unexplained or abnormal drowsiness
- Convulsions or fits
- A severe headache
- Impaired vision

- Vomiting or diarrhoea
- A stiff neck
- Dislike of bright light
- Any severe pain
- Is distressed in any way
- Refusal to eat food for a day or two
- Breathlessness
- Swellings or rash
- Any other unexpected symptoms.

---

1 Salisbury & Begg, Immunisation against infectious disease, Dept of Health, HMSO, 1996.
2 Trevor Gunn, lecture. See chapter 4 for definition of killed and live vaccines.
3 Pollock & Morris, The Lancet 1983: 1: 753-757.
4 The Informed Parent Newsletter, Issue Two, 2002.
5 Salisbury & Begg, op. cit.
6 Salisbury & Begg, op. cit.
7 Charlish. Vaccination and Immunisation. What Does Your Child Need. Thorsons. 1996.

CHAPTER 3

A SHORT WORD ON NUMBERS

Don't worry, we're not going to blind you with statistics, graphs, and probabilities in this chapter. However, throughout the book we will refer to the numbers - normally always government figures - of people who get a disease, of people who die from it, and of children who experience side effects from a disease or vaccination. There are two reasons for this. Firstly, if you see the sorts of numbers involved you can decide for yourself if the risk involved is too high. Secondly, governments use these numbers to devise their policy on immunisation. They are important figures. Having said that, things are not so straightforward. There are many different ways both of gathering the information, and of interpreting the figures.

Gathering information

The incidence of disease in the UK is monitored by the Public Health Laboratory Service (PHLS). The PHLS releases these figures in a table called the Statutory Notification of Infectious Diseases (NOIDS for short). These figures are primarily gathered by doctors reporting a case of an infectious disease to their local public health official who then informs the PHLS. This system is not foolproof, mainly because it relies on the opinion of the local GP who may never have previously seen the disease in question. Many recently qualified doctors have not seen a case of measles, for example.

For some diseases, that is the end of it. In about 50% of cases of a disease like meningitis, a blood sample is sent to a lab to be analysed, and the disease is confirmed. When you see laboratory-confirmed figures, they will always be lower than the true incidence of that disease. This is because they can only reflect the number of cases where blood samples were taken and analyzed. This cannot happen all the time. For example, if the illness must be treated immediately, by the time that blood samples are taken, the antibiotics may have killed off the bacteria.

The true incidence of a disease probably lies nearer the NOIDS figures than the lab figures. Laboratory figures may be inaccurate for any given year, but they do provide a more reliable way of examining trends from year to year.

There are now new systems introduced in the detection of meningitis, for example, aimed at making the reporting of disease even more accurate. The ***enhanced disease surveillance scheme*** was introduced fully in January 1999, and is far more thorough than NOIDS.

Interpreting information

It is worrying that a lot of our and the Government's decisions have to be based on unreliable figures, but hopefully over time, the gathering of information will improve. The main point to be aware of, is when comparisons between years are made, that similar methods were used to obtain the figures you are comparing.

Many articles about the use of vaccinations can be manipulative with the figures. For example most vaccinations are at best 95% effective. This means that if 100 people were given a jab against measles, 95 should not get measles, and 5 should get it, if exposed to the disease. We must bear this in mind when reading some studies. To illustrate this, let's say there was a measles outbreak in Community A. 500 children got measles. Then it was discovered that all of these children had already been vaccinated against measles. Media uproar. But actually, if you look at the bigger picture, you realise that this can be explained by the 95% effectiveness rate of the measles jab. When we look more closely, we see that 10,000 children were given the measles jab in the whole of Community A. Of those 10,000 inoculated children, 500 got measles. In other words, 5% of the children given the jab, got measles. This means the jab is 95% effective.

In Appendix 1, you'll find more numbers to help you when deciding whether to vaccinate your child or not.

CHAPTER 4

WHAT'S IN THE VACCINES?

Live vaccines

MMR and oral polio are made with live versions of the bacteria that lead to the disease. The bacteria are attenuated, or weakened, to make the vaccine less dangerous. When this weakened version of the disease is injected into the blood stream, the body makes antibodies that fight the disease. These antibodies then remain present in the body to fight the real thing, if and when it occurs.

Because the vaccine contains live bacteria, there is a small chance of the disease reproducing itself in the recipient. (See chapter 13 on polio). One study has also found live vaccines may limit your child's growth early on. Infants under six months old, who were immunised with live agents such as polio vaccines, "suffered statistically significant reductions in their weight for age, compared to matched non-immunised controls." [1]

Killed or inactivated vaccines

Killed vaccines are made of components of the disease that are made inactive by heat, radiation or chemicals. Pertussis, Hib and meningitis C are made with killed vaccines. Because the bacteria have been killed, they cannot infect the recipient.

Toxoid vaccines

A toxoid is the poisonous product of a disease organism, which has been rendered harmless by chemical treatment. This is then used in the vaccine to stimulate antibodies, but not the actual illness. Diphtheria and tetanus are both toxoid vaccines.

Throughout this book, we will list the ingredients of the various vaccinations. Here we take a quick look at some of the more familiar, and controversial, vaccine ingredients.

Common substances found in vaccines include:

- **Antibiotics** are added to vaccines to prevent the growth of germs (bacteria) in the vaccine cultures.

- **Formaldehyde** is used to inactivate bacterial products for toxoid vaccines. Formaldehyde is also used to kill unwanted viruses and bacteria that might be found in the vaccine cultures.

- **Thiomersal** (also called thimerosal) is a preservative made from mercury that is sometimes added to prevent the vaccine from spoiling. It is also found in some contact lens solutions and throat sprays. (See below).

- **Aluminium gels or salts of aluminium** are added as adjuvants to help the vaccine to stimulate the production of antibodies to fight off diseases and aid the other vaccine ingredients to do their job.

- **Egg protein** is found in vaccines that are made using chick embryos. If your child has an allergy to eggs, he should not have these vaccines.

- **Suspending fluid** e.g. sterile water, saline or fluids containing protein.

- **Monosodium glutamate** is used as a stabiliser to help the vaccine remain unchanged, even when it is exposed to heat, light, acidity or humidity.

- **Other preservatives and stabilisers** e.g. albumen, phenols and glycine that help the vaccine remain unchanged.

More about Thiomersal

Thiomersal is a controversial ingredient in vaccinations, because it contains 49.6% mercury by weight. It is known as Thimerosal in America. It has been used in very small amounts in vaccines since the 1930s, as it prevents bacterial and fungal contamination. Not all vaccines contain thiomersal.

Mercury causes poisoning only after it reaches a certain level in the body. That level depends on bodyweight, so if an adult and a baby are given the same amount of mercury, the baby will be at greater risk. Mercury poisoning affects the central nervous system, with symptoms such as lethargy, loss of appetite, weight loss, tremor, memory loss, sleep disturbance, confusion, inflammation of the gums, loose teeth and a rash. In the very low doses of thiomersal that is contained in vaccines, there is no evidence that it causes mercury poisoning. However new-born babies, especially those with low bodyweight, who have repeated doses of vaccines containing thiomersal, may end up with a higher than recommended level of mercury. This may lead to the mercury poisoning symptoms described above. Symptoms of mercury poisoning are in many cases identical to the symptoms of autism.[2] However, a recent study in the Lancet found that thiomersal-containing vaccines do not raise the level of mercury in the blood.[3]

In the USA it was calculated that if all thiomersal-containing childhood vaccines were given, the total exposure to mercury in the first six months of life may exceed the U.S. Environmental Protection Agency guidelines. The Immunization Safety Review Committee in the United States reviewed the safety of thiomersal in vaccines. The committee could not prove a link between thiomersal and neurological and developmental problems, but it concluded that such a link is biologically plausible. Two other recent studies could also find no link.[4] The committee recommended that thiomersal be removed from all vaccines.[5] As a result, all thiomersal vaccines in the States were withdrawn, and all standard vaccinations currently being manufactured for America, contain no thiomersal or only trace amounts of thiomersal. The European Medicines Evaluation Agency has also recommended phasing out the use of thiomersal, as a precaution.

The only vaccines in the UK's childhood immunisation programme that contain thiomersal are those for DTaP and DTP-Hib, and the diphtheria/tetanus booster. It is not used in MMR, polio, meningitis C or BCG.[6]

Animal Links

Animal cells are often used to make vaccines, and there is concern that some diseases previously confined to certain animal species, are now being seen in humans. For example, SV40 may have been passed onto children by using infected monkey cells in a polio vaccine. (See chapter 13). And senior government advisors in the UK have said, as early as 1989, that vaccinations can provide a route by which BSE can be transferred to human beings. Foetal bovine serum (which comes from cows) is widely used for growing vaccinations, such as DTP. If the serum comes from BSE infected cows, then it has the potential to produce a vaccination that might infect humans with vCJD.[7]

---

1 American Journal of Clinical Nutrition 1977; 30:592-8.
2 The Informed Parent, Issue 2, 2000.
3 The NHS website www.immunisation.org.uk, 16th January 2003.
4 www.immunisation.org.uk, op. cit.
5 Stratton et al, Immunization Safety Review: Thimerosal-containing vaccines and Neurodevelopmental disorders, Institute of Medicine, 2001.
6 www.immunisation.org.uk, op. cit
7 Susan Curtis. Homoeopathic Alternatives to Immunisation. Winter Press. 2002.

CHAPTER 5

MENINGITIS C

What is meningitis?

Meningitis is an inflammation of the membranes covering the brain and spinal cord. There are two types - viral and bacterial. Viral meningitis isn't usually very serious and clears up on its own without treatment. Bacterial meningitis is very serious, and can be fatal if not treated promptly. There are at least 50 kinds of bacteria that cause meningitis. The most common ones are:

- ***Meningococcal bacteria:*** These bacteria now cause most cases of bacterial meningitis in Britain.[1] Meningococcal infection can lead to meningitis, septicaemia (blood poisoning) or both. Both diseases are extremely dangerous. In England and Wales, about 200 people a year die from meningococcal infection.[2] We will consider meningococcal bacteria in more detail in a moment.

- ***Pneumococcal bacteria:*** These are the second biggest cause of bacterial meningitis in Britain. They more often cause earache, pneumonia and other less serious illnesses. More on this later.

- ***Haemophilus influenzae B (Hib):*** These bacteria used to be the most common cause of meningitis in children under 5, but cases dropped by 90% after the introduction of the Hib vaccine in 1992.[3] However there has been a small increase of Hib meningitis cases recently. See chapter 6.

- ***Group B Streptococcal (GBS):*** These bacteria are the main cause of meningitis in newborn babies. Up to 90% of babies who get this form of meningitis survive, and half of those suffer no significant after effects.[4]

Meningococcal Bacteria

As we've already stated, these bacteria are the most common cause of meningitis in Britain today. There are several types of these bacteria, but in the UK, there are only two major groups that cause the disease:

- ***Group B:*** Meningitis caused by this group of bacteria is known more commonly as meningitis B, and accounts for 60-65% of meningitis cases. It is the most deadly strain of meningitis, and as yet there is no vaccine.
- ***Group C:*** These lead to meningitis C (30-35% of cases). The **meningitis C** vaccine was introduced in 1999/2000. Britain is the first and, at present, only country in the world, to vaccinate against meningitis C.

Another group, Group W135, is on the increase, with over 100 cases per year in the UK. This coincides with outbreaks amongst pilgrims to Mecca, and close family contacts in the UK of these pilgrims have often been affected.[5]

Many of the meningitis-causing bacteria that we have discussed live harmlessly in the mucus in the back of the nose and throat in 1 in 10 of the population and in up to 1 in 4 young adults in schools, colleges and military barracks.[6] Most people are not affected by the bacteria at all and are simply carriers with no symptoms. Indeed these bacteria may prevent more dangerous types of meningococcal bacteria getting into the body. However, if the immune system is weak, the bacteria can pass either into the bloodstream, and cause septicaemia (blood poisoning), or into the brain causing meningitis. We do not know what makes certain people susceptible. The bacteria are weak and don't live outside the body for more than a few minutes, so meningitis is only spread by close contact.

Infection by meningococcal bacteria is extremely dangerous. Between 1975 and 1995, almost 1 in 10 of those people who were infected with the bacteria, died.[7] As we've already mentioned, meningococcal bacteria can cause meningitis, septicaemia or both. Both can be fatal if not treated immediately. Here we list the symptoms of each disease. If you suspect your child has either disease, get medical help immediately.

Symptoms of bacterial meningitis

Bacterial meningitis symptoms come on very suddenly, so prompt action is vital. Your child will have some or all of the following: a high fever with vomiting, a severe headache or a stiff neck. He'll start shivering, and have cold hands and feet. He'll begin rapid breathing, be intolerant to light, feel drowsy, he'll have stomach and joint pains and a rash. In babies you may also see a bulging fontanelle, (the soft spot on top of his head). His body will be stiff with jerking movements, and he'll give a fretful shrill cry if disturbed. He'll suffer a loss of appetite and have pale blotchy skin.

Symptoms of septicaemia

If the bacteria enter your child's bloodstream, they rapidly cause septicaemia, which is very dangerous. Septicaemia causes the red blotchy rash under the skin, which can be tested for using the 'Glass Test'. Press a glass tumbler onto your child's skin over the rash. If the skin remains red despite the pressure, then this is a sure sign of septicaemia and very fast action must be taken.

Symptoms of viral meningitis

Viral meningitis is much milder than bacterial meningitis. Symptoms include fever, headache, vomiting and nausea. It is like a bad case of flu, and as we've said, will clear up on its own but always get a diagnosis from your doctor.

What is the treatment for meningitis or septicaemia?

If you suspect your child has meningitis or septicaemia, you must go to hospital IMMEDIATELY, where antibiotics will normally be given while the situation is assessed. The earlier the treatment is given the better the chances of your child's survival. About one in every twenty people with meningitis, and one in five people with septicaemia will die.[8]

What is the risk of my child contracting meningitis or septicaemia?

As we have already mentioned, many people carry the various bacteria that can lead to meningitis or septicaemia in the back of their throats. They are spread by coughs and sneezes. However it is not known what makes a carrier of these bacteria susceptible to developing the disease. All we do know is that children under five, and adolescents are the most susceptible groups.

The diseases are seasonal, with more cases of meningitis and septicaemia in winter, and also cyclical. There are years when the diseases are rare, and years when they are common. There were epidemics during the two world wars, and then a pretty steady lull until the latest epidemic, which began in 1985. The number of cases has continued to rise since then, leading to the highest peak for 50 years, at the end of the 1990s, although some of this increase may be down to improved diagnosis.[9 10]

In England, currently, about 1 person in every 10,000 contracts a form of meningococcal meningitis or septicaemia,[11] and most cases are isolated events. The outbreaks in schools that you hear about in the news from time to time tend to be meningitis C, but since the introduction of the meningitis C vaccine, these outbreaks are much rarer.[12]

What can I do to protect my child from meningitis or septicaemia?

In 1999 the Government introduced a vaccine to protect people against meningitis C. We will discuss its efficacy in a moment, but remember that before the vaccine was introduced the Group C bacteria accounted for around 30% of cases of meningitis in the UK. Group B bacteria cause about 60 - 65% of meningitis cases. There is still no vaccine to protect children against Group B bacteria or many other equally deadly forms of meningitis and septicaemia. Because of this, it is vital that you are able to recognise the symptoms of these diseases (see above) and get medical help immediately.

There is now also a vaccine for ***pneumococcal meningitis,*** intended for those most at risk (consult your doctor), although the UK Government is considering adding it to the general vaccination programme, once proper evaluation has been carried out.

When should my child have the meningitis C vaccine?

It is given at 2, 3 and 4 months by injection.

How well will the meningitis C vaccine protect my child?

The meningitis C vaccine was introduced in the UK in November 1999 to protect against Group C meningitis and septicaemia. Before its introduction, about 150 people each year died from Group C meningitis and septicaemia in the UK.[13] In the first 9 months of 1999, up until the vaccination was started, there were 47 deaths from confirmed cases of meningitis C. In the same period in 2001 there were just three deaths.[14]

Table 2: Number of cases of Group C meningitis in England & Wales 1990 - 2001.[15]

Year	Number of cases
1990	467
1991	393
1992	328
1993	318
1994	290
1995	461
1996	605
1997	813
1998	811
1999*	982
2000	711
2001	319

* Meningitis C vaccine introduced in November 1999.

The vaccine has been offered to almost everyone aged eighteen and under in the UK, and cases of the Group C disease in these targeted age groups have dropped by over 85%.[16] The under-one's and 15 to 19-year-olds have shown the biggest falls. In 1999, 105 under-one's were infected by the Group C bacteria. In 2000, this figure had dropped to 30 - a fall of 71%. 192 teenagers aged 15 to 19 contracted the Group C disease in 1999, compared with 67 in 2000.

Group C meningitis and septicaemia continued to rise in the 20 to 24-year-olds, so the vaccine programme was extended to include all under-25's, in January 2002.[17] As more and more people are given the meningitis C vaccine, the impact of the immunisation programme "is expected to improve".[18]

The Government states that tests done on the vaccine indicate that it should produce long-lasting immunity.[19] We are not clear how these tests are carried out, considering the vaccine has only been in existence for a relatively short time.

When should my child NOT have the meningitis C vaccine?

Doctors recommend that the vaccine should not be given, if your child

- Is allergic to any part of the vaccine,
- Has a fever or is ill with anything,
- Has a history of childhood fits,
- Is pregnant or is a breast-feeding mother,
- Has had a serious reaction to a previous dose of the vaccine,
- Has thrombocytopenia or any other blood disorder.

Furthermore, alternative practitioners recommend that a vaccine should also not be given, if your child

- Has had a previous reaction to any vaccine.

What's in the meningitis C vaccine?

Meningitis C vaccine contains meningococcal Group C oligosaccharide and corynebacterium; diphtheriae CRM protein; aluminium phosphate; sodium chloride and water. The vaccine is not live, so cannot cause a mild form of meningitis or septicaemia.[20]

What are the side effects of the meningitis C vaccine?

Before it was introduced, the meningitis C jab was tested on 25,000 people. Since then it has been administered to more than 15 million children. The Department of Health lists the following side effects from the vaccine: [21]

- Redness and swelling at injection site,
- 1 in 20 may get a mild fever,

- disturbed sleep,
- extremely sore arm for a few days,
- irritability and
- headaches.

Other side effects have been reported by parents:

- Crying,
- drowsiness,
- anorexia,
- diarrhoea,
- vomiting and
- myalgia (pain in the muscles).

Between 1st November 1999 and July 2000 there have been nearly 5,000 reports of side effects in children. The most common appear to be blackouts and severe persistent headaches that last for weeks.[22] According to the Meningitis Research Foundation, one in every half a million doses produces a serious allergic reaction, but it is not fatal.[23]

16 children have died after having the meningitis C vaccine but there is no proof that the deaths were related to the jab.[24]

Meningitis B and Hib

Laboratory tests have confirmed that bacteria from the meningitis C vaccine can mutate into the meningitis B form, and infect both the recipient of the jab, and their close contacts, with meningitis B. Researchers are currently studying a group of 15,000 teenagers to discover whether the meningitis C vaccination triggers the most deadly strain of meningitis - meningitis B.[25] Group B meningitis and septicaemia have been on the rise in the UK, especially in children,[26] since the mid-1990s. See Table 3, below.

Table 3: Number of cases of Group B meningitis and of all meningococcal meningitis in England & Wales, 1989 - 2001.[27]

Year	Number of cases of Group B meningitis	Total number of cases of meningococcal meningitis
1989	884	1,353
1990	994	1,497
1991	961	1,398
1992	921	1,301
1993	930	1,299
1994	789	1,128
1995	906	1,443
1996	841	1,844
1997	1,157	2,455
1998	1,193	2,425
1999*	1,462	2,783
2000	1,642	2,653
2001	1,688	2,326

*The meningitis C vaccine was introduced in 1999.

Table 3 also shows us that the overall number of cases of meningococcal disease (Groups B, C and all the others) peaked in 1999, and has since decreased. This decrease could be due to the meningitis C vaccine, or be a part of the naturally occurring disease cycles we mentioned earlier.

A more reliable measure of the trends of meningococcal disease can be gained using figures from the enhanced surveillance scheme. This scheme has only been running since 1999. That year there were 4,980 cases of meningococcal disease in England, Wales and Northern Ireland. In 2001 the figure had fallen to 3,627 cases.

The incidence of meningococcal disease in Europe has also dropped from 7,532 cases in 1999, to 5,670 in 2000.[28] Don't forget that Britain is the only country that uses the meningitis C vaccine.

The number of cases of Hib meningitis has begun to rise since 1998. There is a theory that this too could be linked to the meningitis C vaccine. (See chapter 6 for more about Hib).

---

1 Meningitis Research foundation website: www.meningitis.org.uk
2 Communicable Disease Surveillance Centre, 1999/2000 Review.
3 www.meningitis.org.uk, op. cit.
4 www.meningitis.org.uk, op. cit.
5 www.meningitis.org.uk, op. cit.
6 Public Health Laboratory Service website - www.phls.org.uk - April 2002.
7 Salisbury & Begg, Immunisation against infectious disease, Dept. of Health, HMSO, 1996.
8 Salisbury & Begg, op. cit.
9 Communicable Disease Surveillance Centre, op. cit.
10 www.meningitis.org.uk, op. cit.
11 Communicable Disease Surveillance Centre, op. cit.
12 www.meningitis.org.uk, op. cit.
13 A new guide to childhood immunisations, Health Promotion England, and the NHS. 2001.
14 www.info.doh.gov.uk/doh - from a Department of Health press release dated 4/1/2002.
15 Public Health Laboratory Service website - www.phls.org.uk - April 2002.
16 www.meningitis.org.uk, op. cit.
17 www.meningitis.org.uk, op. cit.
18 Communicable Disease Surveillance Centre, op. cit.
19 Department of Health website factsheet: "The New Meningitis C Vaccine", November 1999.
20 www.meningitis.org.uk, op. cit.
21 Vaccine fact-sheet, Department of Health 1999.
22 The Vaccine Awareness Network website - www.vaccine-info.com
23 www.meningitis.org.uk, op. cit.
24 Government figures quoted in The Guardian, op. cit.
25 Karpasea-Jones, Everything There is To Know About Vaccination, A Vaccine Information Services Publication, 2002.
26 www.meningitis.org.uk, op. cit.
27 Public Health Laboratory Service website, op. cit.
28 Communicable Disease Surveillance Centre, op. cit.

CHAPTER 6

DTP-HIB AND DTAP

DTP-Hib is a quadruple vaccine protecting against diphtheria, tetanus, pertussis (which is whooping cough) and the Hib bacteria. A quadruple jab ensures more people are protected, than if each vaccine were given separately, and so herd protection will be more easily achieved. The jab is given to 2, 3 and 4-month-olds.

DTaP is the booster jab, given to pre-schoolers, to boost their immunity against diphtheria, tetanus and pertussis. It contains a different type of pertussis vaccine. We will discuss the difference in chapter 10.

First we will look at the diseases. Then we will consider the vaccinations.

HAEMOPHILUS INFLUENZAE B (HIB)

What is Hib?

Haemophilus influenzae type B (or Hib for short) is not actually a disease. It is a bacterium that can cause various diseases and is most harmful in children from 3 months to 4 years old. It has been shown to be an important cause of childhood meningitis and a major cause of bacterial pneumonia in children.

The Hib bacteria live harmlessly in the mucus in the back of the nose and throat of 1 in 10 people. If the immune system is weak, the bacteria can pass into the blood system and the brain. It is spread by close contact, such as coughs and sneezes, or, for example, if you wipe children's noses with the same hanky, nasal mucus is passed from one child to the other.

Hib most commonly leads to meningitis (in approximately 60% of cases); epiglottitis in 15% of cases (a potentially dangerous swelling of the air passages, restricting your child's breathing); and septicaemia, or blood poisoning in 10% of cases.

Other illnesses caused by Hib infection are septic arthritis, osteomyelitis (inflammation of the bone), cellulitis (inflammation of the tissues under the skin), pneumonia and pericarditis (inflammation of the protective membrane of the heart).[1]

What are the symptoms of Hib meningitis?

For symptoms of meningitis and septicaemia, see page 22.

What is the treatment for Hib?

You will need to get your child to hospital immediately. She will then be treated with a course of antibiotics. If treatment begins early enough, recovery is usually good. A small proportion of children who are not treated early enough will die from the disease. Nowadays, 95% of people with Hib meningitis survive. In 1999, only one person died from Hib meningitis.[2] Of those who survive, some have serious and lasting disabilities. This may include deafness, mental deficiency, cerebral palsy and epilepsy,[3] although antibiotics may reduce the chance of deafness.[4] One UK study showed that about 1 in 10 Hib sufferers were left with permanent brain damage.[5]

What is the risk of my child catching Hib meningitis or another Hib infection?

As with meningitis, many people carry the Hib bacteria in their throats, but very few actually fall ill. Those that do are thought to be people with a deficient immune system, people without a spleen, those with chronic lung disease or liver damage.

Before the introduction of the routine Hib vaccination, one in every 600 children were infected by Hib before their fifth birthday,[6] and half of all Hib cases occurred in the under-one's, with the most cases in six to seven-month-olds. The disease is rare in babies younger than three months, probably because they have natural immunity from infection until they are six months old.[7]

Since the Hib vaccine was introduced in 1992, the incidence of Hib meningitis has dropped by 90%. The number of people carrying the bacteria has also dropped, so there is less chance of someone who has not been immunised, actually picking up the bacteria.[8]

Table 4: Number of cases of Hib meningitis in 1990 - 2001.[9]

Year	Number of cases
1990	431
1991	417
1992*	484
1993	168
1994	52
1995	51
1996	57
1997	38
1998	29
1999	29
2000	39
2001	74

*Hib vaccine introduced

Table 5: Breakdown by age, of Hib meningitis cases, for 2001.[10]

Age range	No. of cases
0 - 1 year	14
1 - 4 years	22
5 - 9	9
10 - 14	4
15 - 24	4
25 - 44	11
45 - 64	6
65+	3
Not known	0

1 Salisbury & Begg, Immunisation against infectious disease, Dept. of Health, HMSO, 1996.
2 Communicable Disease Surveillance Centre, 1999/2000 Review.
3 Welford H, The Complete Book of Child Health, Marshall Cavendish, 1995.
4 U B Schaad , The Lancet 1993; 342: 457-461.
5 Salisbury & Begg, op. cit.
6 Salisbury & Begg, op. cit.
7 Neustaedter, The Immunization Decision. North Atlantic Books, California. 1990.
8 Meningitis Research foundation website: www.meningitis.org.uk
9 Figures from Statutory Notification of Infectious Diseases (NOIDS). England & Wales.
10 NOIDS. England & Wales.

CHAPTER 7

DIPHTHERIA - THE "D" IN DTP-HIB

What is diphtheria?

Diphtheria is a highly contagious bacterial infection that generally affects your throat, but can affect your skin. Your child would contract diphtheria by being in direct contact with someone who has diphtheria or is carrying the diphtheria bacteria. She could also contract diphtheria by drinking contaminated milk.

Symptoms appear two to six days after your child is first infected by the bacteria. She will have a sore throat, a general feeling of weakness and a mild fever. Later, a soft grey membrane will form across her throat. This will restrict the air passages, making it difficult for your child to breathe or swallow. 50% of patients that reach this stage will die. The glands in your child's neck will swell, her breathing will become noisy, her voice husky, and her breath foul-smelling. Bacterial toxins are released into the blood. These cause headaches, a possible red rash and tiredness. Death from heart failure or collapse can follow within four days.

Deaths from diphtheria in the Western world are now extremely rare. There has been one death in the UK, between 1985 and 1999.[1] This was a 14-year-old boy who had visited Pakistan, and had no record of immunisation.[2]

What is the treatment for diphtheria?

Diphtheria is successfully treated with antibiotics. Complete recovery requires prolonged bed rest.

What is the risk of my child contracting diphtheria?

Diphtheria is now rare in most Western countries. In England and Wales there have been twelve cases on average each year for the last few years, although there has been a slight increase since 1992. The Government states that this is due to a less serious version of diphtheria, which tends to show as a sore throat.[3]

Table 6. Breakdown of diphtheria cases in England & Wales, by age, for the year 2001.[4]

Age range	Number of cases
0 - 1 year	0
1 - 4 years	0
5 - 9	0
10 - 14	3
15 - 24	5
25 - 44	4
45 - 64	1
65+	0
Not known	0

95% of all children under two in the UK received the diphtheria vaccine in the year 1999/2000. This is the level needed for herd protection.[5] (See chapter 1).

The disease has been virtually eliminated in the UK, but there are still a few cases imported from abroad. As children are no longer getting natural immunity to diphtheria, health officials feel the jab is necessary to protect against a resurgence of overseas cases of diphtheria that may come into Britain.[6]

1 Public Health Laboratory Service website, www.phls.org.uk.
2 Salisbury & Begg. Immunisation against infectious disease, Dept. of Health, HMSO, 1996.
3 Salisbury & Begg, op. cit.
4 Figures from Statutory Notification of Infectious Diseases (NOIDS).
5 National Statistics. Social Trends No 32: 2002 edition.
6 Salisbury & Begg, op. cit.

CHAPTER 8

TETANUS - THE "T" IN DTP-HIB

What is tetanus?

Tetanus (or lockjaw) is an infectious bacterial disease that affects the nervous system. It is caused when an open cut is contaminated by tetanus bacteria, found in the soil, in animal faeces, in the dust and dirt of towns and cities, in gravel and in rusty metal. Tetanus cannot live in oxygen so the wound has to be deep or dirty for the bacteria to get a hold - and the deeper and dirtier the cut, the more dangerous. Your child will suffer symptoms any time from four to twenty-five days after infection. He will have stiff muscles, first in his jaw (hence the name lockjaw) then his neck and back, followed by his chest, abdomen and limbs. He will often suffer a high fever and convulsions, and will be in extreme pain. If your child is left untreated, the death rate is high, but prompt treatment with penicillin and an anti-toxin is effective.

What is the treatment for tetanus?

If tetanus is diagnosed, your child should go to hospital, where a booster injection of anti-tetanus vaccine will be given. If the disease is not successfully treated at this stage, your child is given large doses of antibiotics and anti-toxins and kept under sedation. He may have to be in intensive care and on a respirator for several weeks. With the right treatment most children recover from tetanus.

What is the risk of my child contracting tetanus?

In developed countries tetanus is very rare. Between 1984 and 1995 there were no cases of tetanus in the UK in children under five years of age, and only three cases in children aged 5 to 14.[1] In 2001, no-one under the age of 25 contracted tetanus in England or Wales, and nobody died from it.[2] It most commonly affects the over-45's. Between 1984 and 1995 three quarters of the cases of tetanus in the UK were in the over-45's.[3]

The National Vaccination Information Centre states, in their Tetanus Fact Sheet, that if the wound is kept clean and aired, the chances of catching tetanus are virtually impossible.

30% of worldwide tetanus cases are caused by umbilical stump infections in newborn babies. This is not a danger in this country, so homoeopaths question why we give the tetanus injection so young.

---

1 Salisbury & Begg. Immunisation against infectious disease, Dept. of Health, HMSO, 1996.
2 Figures from Statutory Notification of Infectious Diseases (NOIDS).
3 Salisbury & Begg, op. cit.

CHAPTER 9

PERTUSSIS - THE "P" IN DTP-HIB

Pertussis is the medical name for whooping cough

What is whooping cough?

Whooping cough is an infectious bacterial disease that mainly affects children. It is spread by coughing and sneezing.

Symptoms will appear one to two weeks after your child has contact with whooping cough. They include catarrh, mild fever, coughing and loss of appetite, and can last for one to two weeks. Your child will then suffer coughing fits, in the form of a series of short coughs followed by an involuntary drawing in of breath. This produces the whooping sound that gives the cough its name. The coughing is usually worse at night and after feeding. Sometimes this coughing can be followed by bleeding from your child's nose and mouth, and also by vomiting. This stage lasts two weeks, and she is infectious throughout.

Over the following two to three weeks, the symptoms slowly decline, but the cough may persist for many weeks. Very rarely, whooping cough leads to severe complications, which are listed below.

Babies, particularly premature babies, are the most vulnerable to whooping cough, as it seems that they do not get natural immunity from their mothers.[1] In children under two years old, death will result in 1 to 2 % of whooping cough cases.[2] The peak age for whooping cough is three years, but for children over two years old, it is not a life-threatening illness, with only about 1% of cases needing hospitalisation. If your child gets whooping cough, she will be infectious for about a month after symptoms first appear, so it is important to keep her isolated from infants.

The worst cases of whooping cough are seen in countries where there is a poor standard of living.

Whooping cough complications

- Fatalities are very rare in children over 6 months of age.
- Pneumonia affects 1 in 100 whooping cough children, and can lead to permanent lung damage.
- Pneumothorax (a collapsed lung).
- Bronchiectasis (a widening of the airways to the lungs).
- Middle ear inflammation.
- Encephalitis (a swelling of the brain).[3]

What is the treatment for whooping cough?

Antibiotics are not very effective, but are prescribed to stop any further infections, and to limit the period during which your child is infectious. There is no real cure apart from time.

What is the risk of my child contracting whooping cough?

Table 7: The number of whooping cough cases and resulting deaths in England & Wales, 1990 - 2001.[4]

Year	Number of cases	Deaths	Deaths per case (%)
1990	15,266	7	0.05
1991	5,201	0	0
1992	2,309	1	0.04
1993	4,091	0	0
1994	3,964	3	0.08
1995	1,869	2	0.11
1996	2,387	2	0.08
1997	2,989	1	0.03
1998	1,577	4	0.25
1999	1,139	2	0.18
2000	712	2*	0.28
2001	886	N/a	-

* Up to September 2000

- Six of the seven deaths in 1990 were in babies under four months of age.
- Five of the deaths between 1991 and 1995 were in babies too young to be immunised.[5]

Table 8: Breakdown of whooping cough cases in England & Wales, by age, for the year 2001.[6]

Age range	Number of cases
0 - 1 year	300
1 - 4 years	200
5 - 9	227
10 - 14	69
15 - 24	21
25 - 44	35
45 - 64	18
65+	3
Not known	13

1 Charlish. Vaccination and Immunisation. What Does Your Child Need. Thorsons. 1996.
2 http://www.faqs.org/faqs/misc-kids/vaccinations/part2.
3 Charlish, op. cit.
4 Figures from Statutory Notification of Infectious Diseases (NOIDS).
5 Salisbury & Begg. Immunisation against infectious disease, Dept of Health, HMSO, 1996.
6 NOIDS.

CHAPTER 10

DIPHTERIA, TETANUS, PERTUSSIS AND HIB:

THE VACCINATIONS

If your child follows the Government's immunisation schedule, he will have the DTP-Hib quadruple jab at two, three and four months. Then he will have the pre-school booster of DTaP at any age from three to five. He will also have a diphtheria/tetanus booster on leaving school.

DTP or DTaP - what's the difference?

DTP stands for diphtheria, tetanus, pertussis. DTaP stands for diphtheria, tetanus and attenuated pertussis. The pertussis vaccine in DTP is made from the whole cell of the pertussis bacterium, and is called a "whole cell" vaccine. The attenuated pertussis vaccine, in DTaP, is weaker, and is made from part of the bacterium. It's called an acellular vaccine. We still use both vaccines in the UK.

According to the NHS, the whole cell DTP vaccine provides better protection. The side effects of DTP and DTaP are similar for babies of 2, 3 or 4 months of age, but DTP has more severe side effects for older children. Because of this, the Government recommends the DTP vaccine for the 2, 3 and 4 months jabs, as it gives your child better protection. The DTP is not recommended for pre-school children because of its side effects for children of that age. Instead the Government recommends using the DTaP vaccine, which although weaker than DTP, will be adequate to provide the necessary boost to your child's immunity to whooping cough, tetanus and diphtheria.[1]

What do other countries do?

The Americans and seven European countries (including Germany, Sweden and Ireland)[2] have switched to using DTaP as they believe there are fewer side effects than with the DTP jab. However it is thought that DTaP, which costs more, may not provide as much protection against whooping cough. Many countries are sticking with the DTP as it costs less, and is considered to be more efficient.[3]

What are the alternatives to having the multiple jabs?

If you are worried about the multiple jabs, but you still want your child protected against some or all of the diseases, then it is possible to have some of the vaccines separately. Your child can have Hib at one time, or in one arm, and then have DTP later or in the other arm. You may decide not to have the pertussis jab at all. If so, you can have a diptheria/tetanus (DT) double jab, although you may need a good reason not to have the pertussis jab at the same time. Tetanus is also available singly but only as a booster for older children.

The Government does not recommend these options. First, the longer you take to vaccinate your child, the longer you are leaving him exposed to the diseases. Second, the Government is keen to vaccinate as many children as possible. It fears that if you split the jabs up, fewer children will complete the course.

If you did want to go down this route, you would need to talk to your doctor. As it is not part of the government schedule, your surgery may not be willing or able to offer the jabs separately.

What's in the DTP-Hib vaccine?

DTP contains diphtheria bacterium, killed pertussis organisms, tetanus toxoid, and is produced using aluminium hydroxide and thiomersal.[4] Thiomersal is a mercury derivative, discussed in chapter 4.

The Hib vaccine is cultured in cattle tissue and also contains thiomersal, phenol, bacterial polysaccharides, polyribosylribitol, and ammonium sulphate.[5]

What's in the DTaP vaccine?

DTaP contains diphtheria bacterium, pertussis organisms, tetanus toxoid, and can be produced using formaldehyde, aluminium hydroxide, aluminium phosphate, polysorbate 80, gelatin and thiomersal.

What's in the DT vaccine?

Diphtheria and tetanus toxoids, aluminium phosphate and thiomersal. This is suitable for children under 6 for whom simultaneous pertussis vaccination is not advised.[6]

Why does my child need a quadruple jab at such a young age?

Whooping cough (pertussis) is only really fatal to children under six months of age, so the jab is introduced at two months. Likewise, infection from Hib bacteria occurs mainly in the very young. The WHO recommends giving the vaccine "as early in life as possible." [7] The Hib vaccine is not recommended for children over 4 years of age.[8]

When should my child NOT have the DTP-Hib vaccine?

Doctors recommend that the vaccine should not be given, if your child

- Is allergic to any part of the vaccine,
- Has a fever or is ill with anything,
- Is pregnant or is a breast-feeding mother,
- Has thrombocytopenia or any other blood disorder,
- Has a history of childhood fits, although the manufacturer's insert that comes with the vaccine disagrees. It says that if your child has a personal or family history of febrile convulsions (fits), he can still have the jabs, but you should take advice on how to prevent a fever. This is because there is an increased risk of your child having febrile convulsions after the pertussis element of the jab.[9]

If your child did have a serious reaction at the site of the injection to the previous dose of DTP-Hib, doctors recommend that he should continue with the jabs, but have the DTP jab in a different part of his body from the Hib. If he had a serious generalised reaction (that is one not specifically at the site of the injection), then he should have Hib and DT only (not pertussis), again at different points on his body.[10] The pertussis element of DTP-Hib is the most likely to cause side effects.

Alternative practitioners recommend that a vaccine should not be given, if your child has had a previous reaction to *any* vaccine.

If your child has an evolving neurological disease, he should wait to have the jab until his condition is stable. If your child has a stable neurological disease such as cerebral palsy or spina bifida, he can have the DTP-Hib jab.

---

1 The NHS website www.immunisation.org.uk.
2 Therre and Baron, Eurosurveillance Monthly, 2000; 5: 6-10
3 Gangarosa et al, Lancet 1998; 351: 356-61.
4 Pasteur Merieux website.
5 www.whale.to/vaccines/ingredients.
6 Connaught vaccine manufacturer information sheet.
7 WHO website
8 Salisbury & Begg, Immunisation against infectious disease, Dept. of Health, HMSO, 1996.
9 Pasteur Merieux MSD Ltd, January 1995
10 Salisbury & Begg, op. cit.

CHAPTER 11

THE EFFECTIVENESS OF THE DTP-HIB AND DTAP VACCINES

The quadruple vaccine is a recent introduction to Britain's immunisation programme. Previously Hib was administered separately to DTP, and earlier still, diphtheria, tetanus and pertussis were administered individually. The quadruple vaccine is four single vaccines rolled into one. There are theories that a compound vaccine such as this one may reduce the effectiveness of the individual components,[1] and may increase the chance of side effects. For example, some research has pointed out that giving Hib at the same time as DTP can reduce the effectiveness of the DTP jab.[2]

How well does the diphtheria element of the vaccine protect my child?

In England and Wales, death rates from diphtheria have been falling since the turn of last century (see Table 9 below). Widespread diphtheria vaccination began in Britain in 1941.[3] As you can see from the table, the death rate continued to fall, until by the 1960s it was virtually zero.

Table 9. Deaths from diphtheria in England & Wales since 1901.[4]

Year	Average number of deaths from diphtheria per year
1901 - 1910	6,092
1911 - 1920	5,048
1921 - 1930	3,270
1931 - 1940	2,884
1941 - 1950*	836
1951 - 1960	13
1961 - 1970	2
1971 - 1978	Less than 1

*Diphtheria vaccination started in Britain in 1941.

Since 1945, the World Health Organisation has measured more than 30,000 cases of diphtheria in British children, who had received the diphtheria vaccine, so having the vaccine does not guarantee immunity.[5] However bear in mind that more than 15 million children have been vaccinated in the UK since 1945 which gives the vaccine an effectiveness level of over 99%. That's a very rough calculation, but it highlights the fact that 30,000 cases of diphtheria since 1945 does not mathematically mean the vaccination is ineffective.

There have been large epidemics recently in Russia and the former Soviet Union. In 1995, there were 52,000 cases with 1700 deaths. These were due to low immunisation coverage, waning immunity in adults and large population movements.[6]

Blood received from blood donors in the UK was measured for its antibodies to diphtheria. More than 1 in 3 blood donors were found to be susceptible to diphtheria, and you are more likely to catch the disease as you get older: 1 in 4 people in their twenties could get diphtheria compared to over half of people in their fifties.[7]

How long does the diphtheria vaccine last?

The diphtheria vaccine lasts ten years.[8] The diphtheria booster is given to protect those children who weren't protected by the first set of vaccinations, or who were never given the first jabs, or whose immunity has waned.

How well does the tetanus element of the vaccine protect my child?

- 97% of children under five have tetanus antibodies in their blood following vaccination. In most cases, this ensures that they are protected from the disease.[9]
- Many studies in America in World War II have shown that the tetanus jab is highly effective, and all recent cases of tetanus in the USA have been in people that haven't had the jab.[10]
- Immunity is not life-long, and booster injections are needed if serious injury occurs. However, the effectiveness of the jab reduces after five boosters have been given.

- Cases of tetanus that have occurred in fully immunised individuals were not fatal.[11]

How well does the pertussis element of the vaccine protect my child against whooping cough?

The Department of Health states that four out of every five children (that's 80%) who have the full course of vaccinations, will be protected from whooping cough.[12]

In 1998 researchers compared data from several countries.[13] They looked at both the incidence rate of whooping cough in each country and what percentage of children were given the whole-cell pertussis vaccine. They concluded that countries with a high level of vaccination had less cases of whooping cough:

- First the researchers looked at Hungary, the former East Germany, and Poland. These three countries have very high coverage levels, with 95% of children given the DTP jab. Each country has consistently reported about one case of whooping cough a year for every 100,000 people.

- In the former West Germany, when vaccination rates were as low as 11%, about 35% of school aged children had whooping cough. The low vaccination rates were attributed to doctors believing that whooping cough was a "normal" childhood illness.

- In Sweden there was a different story. Following fears of side effects of the DTP jab, and doubts raised over how serious pertussis actually is, coverage levels of the DTP vaccine fell from 90% in 1974 to just 12% in 1979. The jab was abandoned in 1979, while they waited for a safer and more effective one to come along. From 1980 to 1983 incidence levels of whooping cough in Sweden reached 3370 per 100,000, although this levelled off to 100 cases per 100,000. In 1996, the acellular vaccine was introduced. Uptake has been high, and the incidence of whooping cough has decreased to 16 cases per 100,000 in 1998. The majority of these cases were in the five to nine age group who had not been given the new vaccine.[14]

- In Japan, after two children died within 24 hours of receiving the DTP jab, the vaccination was banned. Coverage fell from 80% in 1974 to 10% in 1976. In 1979 there was a whooping cough epidemic, with 13,000 cases and 41 deaths. In 1981 Japan brought in the acellular pertussis vaccine and cases of whooping cough have returned to the low levels experienced before 1976.

- In Ireland in 1955, before the pertussis vaccine was introduced, 79 people for every 100,000 suffered from whooping cough. This level dropped to about 10 per 100,000 in the 1970s with immunisation, but then due to opposition to the whole cell vaccine, coverage fell to 30%. There were whooping cough epidemics in Ireland in 1985 and 1989. In the early 1990s coverage was up to 65%, and whooping cough incidence returned to the low levels of the 1970s.

In the UK, the number of people dying from whooping cough has been in steady decline since the turn of the last century. Mass immunisation against whooping cough started in 1957, and the decline continued.

Table 10: Number of deaths in England & Wales from whooping cough since 1900.[15]

Year	Average number of deaths from whooping cough per year
1901 - 1910	9,454
1911 - 1920	6,538
1921 - 1930	4,429
1931 - 1940	1,858
1941 - 1950	670
1951 - 1960*	138
1961 - 1970	23
1971 - 1978	9

*Vaccination started in 1957.

In 1970 a report linked the whooping cough jab with encephalopathy and brain damage. By 1978 only 30% of children under two were immunised against whooping cough. There were large outbreaks of the disease in 1978 and 1982. In the 1977/79 outbreak of whooping cough there were more than

100,000 cases and 36 deaths reported in the UK.[16] Later on, research showed that the vaccine does not cause encephalopathy and brain damage. The uptake levels of the pertussis jab have now reached 94% by 1999/2000.[17] This is close to the level required for herd protection.

In America, since the early 1980s, whooping cough cases have been increasing with peaks every three to four years; however the number of reported cases remains much lower than levels seen in the pre-vaccine era.[18]

Other studies have found that the DTP vaccine is not so effective in protecting against whooping cough:

- Researchers in Italy monitored 14,000 children for 17 months after they had been given even the whole cell (DTP) or the acellular (DTaP) vaccine. They found that DTP was only 36% effective, and had more severe side effects than DTaP, which they found to be 76 - 90% effective.[19]

- A study in Sweden looked at 1000 infants, half of whom were given the whole-cell pertussis vaccine, before it was withdrawn. The other half did not have the jab. The children were monitored for more than two years. The researchers concluded that the vaccine was 71 - 80% efficient.[20]

- Research of a 1977 whooping cough epidemic in a rural community in the Shetland Isles found that 93 children had been immunised, and 46 of them (49%) caught whooping cough. Of the 41 non-immunised children, 18 (44%) caught whooping cough. This is a very small sample, but even so, it seemed to make little difference whether the children had been immunised or not - about half of each group contracted whooping cough.[21]

As you can see many of the research papers contradict each other. We have included them to highlight the uncertainty that surrounds the whole-cell and acellular pertussis vaccinations. The big argument put forward by doctors for the pertussis vaccine is, that imperfect as it maybe, the benefit of preventing whooping cough is worth the risk.

How long does the whooping cough vaccine last?

The vaccine does not seem to protect your child for a long time, with very little immunity found in children ten years after vaccination, but then the disease is only dangerous in young children.[22]

In November 2001, the Government introduced the DTaP whooping cough booster vaccine given to pre-school children. Prior to that, no booster was given as whooping cough is only serious in infants. However the death rate from whooping cough was at least 9 children a year, mostly in babies too young to be immunised. It is thought that these children caught whooping cough from their older siblings. The DTaP booster is designed to prevent older children getting whooping cough, and passing it on to their newborn siblings.[23]

How well does the Hib element of the vaccine protect my child?

The Hib vaccine was introduced as a single vaccine in 1992. Before its introduction, there was an average of 800 cases of Hib disease in children every year, and between 20 and 30 childhood deaths a year. Since 1992, there have been less than 50 cases a year, and in 1995 only one child died from Hib infection.

Table 11 Number of laboratory reported cases of Hib infection in England & Wales, 1983 - 1995.[24]

Year	Number of cases
1983	869
1989	1,259
1992	627 (229 of which were in the under-1's)
1995	39 (9 of which were in the under-1's)

However since 1998 there has been a gradual increase of cases each year. In 2002, there were 122 cases of Hib disease in children. This is why the Government has introduced a six-month Hib booster campaign in 2003. It will involve a booster dose of Hib given to all children aged between six months and four years on 1 April 2003.[25]

Health officials claim that following three doses of DTP-Hib, more than 90% of children will be protected from Hib infection.[26] The WHO says that "following the introduction of Hib conjugate vaccines into routine childhood immunisation programmes in the 1990s, Hib disease has largely disappeared in Western Europe, Canada, United States, Australia and New Zealand." [27] It also says that Hib vaccines "have proven to be highly efficacious and virtually free from side-effects." [28]

In the Gambia, the incidence of pneumonia fell by about 20%, following the introduction of the Hib vaccine.[29]

The Hib vaccine is designed to prevent the invasive Hib bacteria infecting children. Therefore it is not aimed at eradicating one specific disease. To monitor the jab's effectiveness, therefore, we need to look at the level of Hib bacteria being detected in sick children. This is done in the laboratory, and Hib levels, as reported above, have been falling. However, as we discussed in chapter 5 there are two other major types of invasive bacterial infections - pneumococcal, and meningococcal. Many alternative practitioners are concerned that the reduction in the levels of Hib infection could be mirrored by increases in these other invasive bacterial infections. Studies in Australia, Philadelphia, Finland and Iceland all show a rise in either pneumococcal or meningococcal infection. The official figures in the UK show no increase in pneumococcal or meningococcal infection. However, even allowing for the fall in levels of Hib infection, the overall level of invasive bacterial disease has remained constant.[30]

How long does the Hib vaccine last?

The duration of immunity is unknown. However the disease is only dangerous to very young children.

---

1 Corbel, Biologicals 1994; 22: 353 - 360.
2 Lederle Laboratories manufacturer's insert.
3 Research Defence Society website: www.rds-online.org.uk. January 2003.
4 www.whale.to website - (Source: 20th century Mortality CD, Office of National Statistics)
5 Lynne McTaggart. The Vaccination Bible. What Doctors Don't Tell You. 1997.

---

6 Salisbury & Begg. Immunisation against infectious disease, Dept. of Health, HMSO, 1996.
7 Salisbury & Begg, op. cit.
8 http://www.faqs.org/faqs/misc-kids/vaccinations/part2/ 23 January 2003.
9 Lynne McTaggart, op. cit.
10 Neustaedter. The Immunization Decision: North Atlantic Books, California. 1990.
11 Salisbury & Begg, op. cit.
12 Salisbury & Begg, op. cit.
13 Gangarosa et al, Lancet 1998; 351: 356-61.
14 Olin & Hollander, Eurosurveillance Monthly 1999; 4: 128-129.
15 www.whale.to website.
16 Aventis Pasteur MSD website.
17 National Statistics. Social Trends No 32: 2002 edition.
18 Website of the Centers for Disease Control and Prevention - www.cdc.gov - part of the US Department of Health and Human Services.
19 Greco et al, The New England Journal of Medicine 1996; 334: 341-349.
20 Viera Scheibner PhD. Vaccination. 1993.
21 Viera Scheibner PhD, op. cit.
22 http://www.faqs.org/faqs/misc-kids/vaccinations/part2., 23 January 2003.
23 www.info.doh.gov.uk - from a Department of Health press release dated 15/10/2001
24 Salisbury & Begg, op. cit.
25 www.info.doh.gov.uk - a Department of Health press release dated 18/2/2003.
26 Salisbury & Begg, op. cit.
27 WHO, Weekly Epidemiological Record, 1998, 73, 64-71.
28 WHO website
29 WHO, Weekly Epidemiological Record, 1998, op. cit.
30 www.whale.to/v/beattie.html

CHAPTER 12

THE SIDE EFFECTS OF THE DTP-HIB AND DTAP VACCINES

What are the side effects of the DTP-Hib jab?

In the information sheet on DTP-Hib from the NHS,[1] the side effects are shown as follows:

- It is normal for your baby to be miserable within 48 hours of the injection.
- Your baby may develop a fever.
- Sometimes a small lump develops where the injection was given. This lump can last for a few weeks.
- Your baby might have a fit within 48 hours of being given the DTP-Hib vaccine. If this happens, call your doctor immediately. Your baby should recover quickly and completely, and your doctor will decide whether to give her any further doses of the vaccine. The NHS points out that young babies can have fits at any time, so if your child has a fit soon after the vaccination, this may not be linked to the jab.

A 1995 study by the Public Health Laboratory Service found a significant association between the DTP vaccination and febrile convulsions (fits) in infants under one.[2] The researchers concluded that for every 16,000 doses of DTP, one child would have a fit within three days of the jab. The third DTP dose (now given at four months) had the highest risk, with one fit happening for every 8,500 doses. When the third dose used to be given at 10 months of age, four times as many children had fits. Because of this finding, the Department of Health advises against delaying your child's DTP-Hib until after she is four months old, as you'll increase the chances of her having fits.[3]

The side effects listed in the vaccine manufacturer's leaflet for DTP are:

- pain at injection site,
- fever,
- restlessness,
- headache,

- spasms,
- fits,
- high-pitched screaming,
- vomiting,
- anorexia (which is not wanting to eat),
- anaphylactic shock (1 in 16,000 doses),[4]
- Guillain Barré syndrome (numbness and weakness in the limbs, usually with full recovery),
- encephalitis (this is swelling of the brain and happens very rarely) and
- death (extremely rare, although one UK study puts the chances at 1 in 33,000 doses).[5]

According to the manufacturer's insert, serious reactions to the vaccine occur every 1750 doses. If the child is given five doses of diphtheria (at 2, 3 and 4 months, pre- and post-school) then the risk increases fivefold, such that 1 in 350 children would suffer a serious reaction.

More detailed research[6] shows the following frequency of side effects. If your child has a DTP-Hib jab at 2, 3 & 4 months then she has had three doses:

- Fever greater than 38°C experienced for 1 in every 2 doses
- Drowsiness - 1 in 3 doses
- Fretfulness - 1 in 2 doses
- Vomiting - 1 in 5 doses
- Anorexia (not wanting to eat) - 1 in 5 doses
- Persistent and inconsolable crying (for more than three hours) - 1 in 100 doses
- Fever greater than 40.5°C - 1 in 330 doses
- Collapse - 1 in 1750 doses
- Convulsions - 1 in 1750 doses.

What are the side effects of the tetanus element of the jabs?

About 1 person in every 10 given the tetanus jab will experience a reaction of some kind.[7]

The side effects of the tetanus component of the DTP-Hib, DTaP and DT vaccines are:

- Soreness and swelling at the site of injection for up to 10 days,
- fever, headaches, muscle pain and tiredness,
- urticaria (itchy rash),
- anaphylactic (allergic) reaction. If this happens, get medical help immediately, as a shot of adrenaline could save your child's life.
- Guillain Barré syndrome (numbness and weakness in the limbs, usually with full recovery),
- nerve damage to the inner ear,[8]
- very rarely, brachial neuritis (a swelling of the nerves in your arm).[9]
- One manufacturer's leaflet states: "Death has been reported in temporal association with the administration of tetanus toxoid vaccinations".[10] In other words, people have died shortly after receiving a tetanus vaccine, but it hasn't been proved that the vaccine can cause death.

Once your child has had five tetanus injections, she should only be re-vaccinated against tetanus if she suffers a serious injury. Routine boosters of the tetanus vaccine are not needed. There is a risk of side effects, and you'll reduce the effectiveness of the jab if you give it too often.[11]

What are the side effects of the pertussis element of the jabs?

As we have said earlier, the Government realises that the pertussis element of the DTP-Hib jab is likely to be the dangerous part of the vaccine. Many of the side effects of the DTP-Hib jab that we have already listed may well be caused by the pertussis element. Indeed, the manufacturer's insert for DTP states that there is an increased risk of your child having febrile convulsions after the pertussis element of the jab.

Asthma

The pertussis element of the DTP jab has been linked to a rise in childhood asthma. A study in America looked at asthma rates in 446 children. Of the 243 who had been vaccinated with DTP, 26 had asthma (10.6%). Of the 203 children who had not had the pertussis vaccination, but had been vaccinated against other diseases, only 4 had asthma (1.7%). Therefore, significantly more children who had been vaccinated with the pertussis element suffered from asthma.[12] However a study two years later in the same journal concluded that there was no link between the pertussis vaccine and asthma.[13]

Brain Damage
In the 1970s in the UK, reports linked the DTP jab with brain damage. Vaccination rates plummeted, and whooping cough levels rose. However, between 1976 and 1979, when 2 million doses of the DTP vaccine were used, there were no reports of permanent brain damage within 48 hours of the jab.[14]

Following this controversy in the 1970s, the National Childhood Encephalopathy Study was set up. It concluded that the estimated risk of neurological illness within seven days of receiving the DTP jab was one in 110,000 doses, and the risk of still being ill a year after receiving the jab was one in 310,000 doses. The pro-vaccination lobby argues that in many cases the illness would have manifested itself anyway. The anti-vaccination lobby says that the risk of side effects is even higher if you take into account the "soft" neuro-developmental symptoms like learning disorders, attention deficits and behavioural problems.[15] The Government estimates that you are three times less likely to get encephalitis from the jab than from the whooping cough disease itself.[16]

The solicitors, Alexander Harris, are involved in over 100 cases whose parents believe their children have been brain-damaged by DTP.[17]

Cot death
The DTP jab is also linked to cot death (SIDS). Both Wyeth Laboratories and Connaught vaccination manufacturers have stated in their inserts that SIDS (Sudden Infant Death Syndrome) has occurred in infants after a DTP vaccination, but that there is not necessarily a causal connection. A study in America in 1983 looked at 145 cot death victims. 53 of them had been given the DTP vaccination - 27 of them died within four weeks of the shot, 17 within one week, and 6 within 24 hours of receiving the jab.[18] A UK study found two cases of cot death out of 134,700 doses of DTP. One case was within 24 hours, the other within 21 days.[19] The pro-vaccination lobby argues that these results are not proof of a link between DTP and cot death, because most cot death occurs at this age.

Despite this, in America, they have dropped the DTP vaccine and now use DTaP. Researchers compared the side effects of DTP and DTaP by looking at the Vaccine Adverse Reaction Database. They concluded that the DTP jab was 3½ times more likely to lead to death than the DTaP jab, and 76 times more likely to lead to death than the diphtheria/tetanus vaccine alone.[20] Despite this, America's National Vaccine Advisory Committee states that the DTP vaccine is not a proven cause of cot death or brain damage.

There is also evidence that pertussis vaccines can make your child more susceptible to bacterial infections such as Hib or meningococci.[21]

What are the side effects of the Hib vaccine?

- Health officials state that 1 in 10 children will experience swelling and redness, and this will clear up within 24 hours.[22]
- 1 in 50 may experience a fever.
- The WHO refers to a "mild local reaction." [23]
- In 1985 to 1986, there were reports of 152 reactions to the Hib vaccine in the United States, including one death within four hours of the jab. There were also 63 reports of Hib-induced disease shortly after the jab. It's unclear whether those cases were a reaction to the jab, or because the vaccine failed to protect the children in question.[24]

Other side effects of the Hib vaccine include:[25]

- Headache
- Malaise
- Irritability
- Prolonged crying
- Loss of appetite
- Vomiting
- Diarrhoea
- Rash, including urticaria (hives)
- Convulsions
- Transient cyanosis of the lower limbs (bluish colouring when there is not enough oxygen in the blood).

Diabetes

A study in 1997 has found that the timing of the Hib immunisation might have a link to the development of diabetes. Children vaccinated at birth are less likely to develop diabetes than those vaccinated after two months.[26] However a ten year study in Finland monitored more than 100,000 children given the Hib vaccine, and compared them with children born before the vaccine was introduced. The researchers found that it was unlikely that the Hib vaccine caused diabetes, and that there was no more risk of diabetes if the jab was administered at three months of age or at 24 months of age.[27]

1 The NHS website www.immunisation.org.uk. January 2003.
2 Farrington et al, The Lancet 1995; 345:567-9.
3 www.immunisation.org.uk op. cit.
4 Pollock & Morris, The Lancet 1983; 1: 753 - 757
5 Pollock & Morris, op. cit.
6 Taken from www.whale.to/vaccines/dpt1.html.
7 Neustaedter. The Immunization Decision. North Atlantic Books, California. 1990.
8 Charlish. Vaccination and Immunisation. What Does Your Child Need. Thorsons. 1996.
9 Kassianos, Immunization Childhood & Travellers Health, Blackwell Science, 2000.
10 Aventis Pasteur, January 1995.
11 Salisbury & Begg. Immunisation against infectious disease, Dept. of Health, HMSO, 1996.
12 Ellis & Douglas, Journal of the American Medical Association, 1994.
13 Salisbury & Begg, op. cit.
14 Griffith AH, Vaccine 1989;7(3):199-210. Wellcome Research Laboratories.
15 Neustaedter, op. cit.
16 Charlish, op. cit.
17 www.alexharris.co.uk and personal communication.
18 Viera Scheibner PhD. Vaccination. 1993.
19 Pollock & Morris, op. cit.
20 Richard Barr, www.alexharris.co.uk, the website of Alexander Harris Solicitors, 26/4/2002.
21 Viera Scheibner PhD, op. cit.
22 Salisbury & Begg, op. cit.
23 WHO website
24 Neustaedter, op. cit.
25 British National Formulary Number 34 (September 1997), British Medical Association and the Royal Pharmaceutical Society of Great Britain, 1997.
26 Classen & Classen, Infectious Disease Clin Pract, 1997; 6: 449-454.
27 Karvonen et al, BMJ 1999; 318: 1169 - 1172.

CHAPTER 13

POLIO

What is polio?

Poliomyelitis is an infectious viral disease affecting the central nervous system. The virus is found in the faeces (poo) of an infected person, so the disease is most common where sanitation is poor, but as we'll explain, it is most dangerous where sanitation has improved.

Symptoms start 7 to 12 days after infection. There are three different types of polio:

1. Abortive poliomyelitis - where only the throat and intestines (guts) are affected, and the symptoms are those of a stomach upset or flu.

2. Non-paralytic poliomyelitis - where the stomach upset and flu are accompanied by muscle stiffness, particularly in your child's back and neck.

3. Paralytic polio - this is very serious but much less common and occurs in 2% of polio cases. Your child would suffer the symptoms as above, but then he would suffer from weakness and eventual paralysis. 5 to 10% of paralytic polio cases could lead to death.[1] A related disease is bulbar poliomyelitis, when breathing is affected.

Some homoeopaths say that polio is only dangerous to children over three years old. Before this age, your child would only experience abortive polio, with very little risk of it causing paralysis. Your child will then have lifelong immunity from all types of polio. After the age of three, there are possibilities of a serious disease developing, with paralysis, muscle wasting, and even death.[2]

In countries with poor sanitation, polio is widespread, and most children under one are infected with the mild, flu-like, form of the illness. This then gives them immunity for life against the more dangerous paralytic polio.

Ironically, in countries where sanitation has improved, polio is not widespread in the under-one's, so they do not develop natural immunity. They are then at risk of catching the disease later in life, when it could develop into paralytic polio.[3]

What is the treatment for polio?

There is no specific treatment apart from measures to relieve the symptoms.

What is the risk of contracting polio?

- Current statistics say only 10% of people exposed to polio will contract it.[4]
- 95% of children under two in the UK have been immunised against polio.[5] This is the level required for herd protection.
- Since 1993 there been 7 cases of polio in England and Wales:

Table 12: Number of reported cases of polio in England & Wales, 1991-2001.[6]

Year	Number of cases
1991	4
1992	3
1993	1
1994	0
1995	1
1996	1
1997	2
1998	2
1999	0
2000	0
2001	0

- Between 1985 and 1991, 18.4 million doses of the polio vaccine were given to children under fifteen in England and Wales. There were 21 cases of polio in that period, five of which were contracted abroad.[7] The risk of catching polio in the UK is very small.

- In the Netherlands, 71 people from a religious group who had refused the polio vaccine, contracted the disease between September 1992 and February 1993. Of the 71 polio victims, two died, and 59 experienced paralysis of some form. They ranged in age from 10 days to 61 years. The general population, including unvaccinated people, seemed well protected during this outbreak.[8]

Vaccinated people may get polio if the vaccine does not take hold, or if the immunity to polio wears off by adulthood. Furthermore, children living in improved hygienic conditions are less likely to catch mild polio, which would have given them lifelong immunity to all forms of polio.

When does my child have the polio vaccine?

Polio is given at 2, 3 and 4 months by mouth, and a booster before school, and another for school leavers.

When should my child NOT have the polio vaccine?

Common practice in the UK is to have the polio vaccine at the same time as the DTP-Hib jab, but vaccine manufacturers specifically recommend that you don't have a polio vaccination three weeks before or after any other vaccination. Evidence to support this comes from an outbreak of paralytic polio in Germany following a vaccination campaign in the 1980s. The investigation concluded that DTP injections should not be given at the same time as the live polio vaccine, because of the risk of "triggering provocation polio". [9]

Doctors recommend that the vaccine should not be given, if your child

- has an infection, fever, cold etc,
- has a stomach upset, vomiting, diarrhoea,
- is allergic to such antibiotics as penicillin,
- has had a vaccine in the last 3 weeks, or intends having one in the next 3 weeks, (manufacturer's leaflet for a polio vaccine - see above),

- is on hormone replacement therapy,[10]
- is pregnant, or intends to be pregnant in the next 12 weeks,
- is a breast-feeding mother,
- has an immune suppressant illness such as cancer, is on steroids or having radiotherapy or chemotherapy,
- has a family member with an immune suppressant illness.

In these last two cases, your child should be given the non-live polio injection.

How effective is the polio vaccine?

Doctors consider it to be one of the safest and most effective vaccines in use today.[11] In the UK, death rates from polio have decreased over the last century, and are now negligible.

Table 13: Deaths from polio in England & Wales since 1911.[12]

Year	Average number of deaths from polio per year
1911 - 1920	1,247
1921 - 1930	162
1931 - 1940	155
1941 - 1950	300
1951 - 1960*	214
1961 - 1970	28
1971 - 1977	19

*Polio vaccine introduced in the 1950s.

This huge improvement could be due to a number of factors:

1. **The vaccination programme.** The vaccine was introduced in the 1950s, although the death rate had been in serious decline before the introduction of the vaccine.

2. **Improved sanitation levels,** although as we've mentioned, improved sanitation often leads to polio epidemics.
3. **Improved nutrition.**
4. **Redefinition of polio.** In the US, paralytic polio was diagnosed if the patient suffered paralysis for at least 24 hours. The polio vaccine was introduced in America in 1955. After 1955, paralytic polio was diagnosed when a patient suffered paralysis for at least 60 days.[13] This re-definition could account for a drop in the number of reported polio cases.
5. **Mislabelling of diseases.** Many cases that would have been diagnosed as polio are now being called aseptic meningitis (which is a viral meningitis).

What is in the polio vaccine?

The polio vaccine can be taken by mouth (oral vaccine) - on a sugar lump. This is the Sabin vaccine and contains the live polio virus. Alternatively, it is taken by injection - the Salk vaccine. This is a non-live vaccine.

The oral vaccine is the type recommended and given in the UK. It provides better immunity than the non-live vaccine but it does, however, carry a small risk of paralysis (see side effects). In America they switched back to the non-live vaccine in 1995, because they felt the higher risk of the side effects from the oral vaccine could not be justified by the low incidence of the polio disease.

The oral vaccine contains 3 types of live polio virus, as well as magnesium chloride, amino acids, polysorbate 80, purified water, neomycin, sulphate, streptomycin, penicillin, and monkey kidney cell cultures or calf foetus tissues.

The oral vaccine remains active in the bowel for several weeks after the first dose[14] and was introduced to try and remove the severe side effects of the non-live vaccine used at the time (severe convulsions and brain damage).

What are side effects of the polio vaccine?

As we have just said, the live virus will remain active in your child's bowel for 6 to 8 weeks after immunisation. This means polio can be passed on to others through your child's poo. There is one case in the UK each year of a non-vaccinated person contracting polio, by coming into contact with the vaccine in this way.[15]

Unfortunately, one of the strains of virus used to make the vaccine has a very low 'back mutation rate'. As a result, your vaccinated child has a very small risk of contracting full-blown polio. The Government estimates that this happens once in every 1½ million doses of polio administered.[16] In America, the CDC puts the risk at 1 in 500,000 doses. Your child should have four doses of polio by the age of five.

Because of these small risks of polio infection, the live polio vaccine should not be given to anyone who has a weak immune system or who has family members with weak immune systems, such as people undergoing chemotherapy. In these cases the non-live jab should be given. There have been many successful court cases brought in the US, by polio sufferers who were infected in this way.

In 1997, the MMWR Summary of Notifiable Diseases in the US, reported that "since 1980 a total of 147 cases of polio have been reported of which 139 were associated with the use of OPV [the oral live virus]". A recent Secretary of State for Health in the UK has acknowledged that the live vaccine was responsible for 50% of recent new cases of polio in the UK.[17]

Between 1985 and 1991 there were 21 cases of paralytic polio in England and Wales, 13 of which were vaccine-induced. As mentioned earlier, 18.4 million doses of polio were administered to children under 15 in that 6-year period, so there is a very small risk of paralysis caused by a polio vaccine (approximately 1 person paralysed for every 1½ million doses of vaccine.)[18]

Other reported side effects of the polio vaccine include:
- fevers,
- paralysis,
- SV40 cancers (brain tumours),
- lower motor neurone weakness,
- encephalitis (swelling of the brain),
- meningitis,
- fits,
- death.[19]

SV40

SV40 is a cancer that mainly affects monkeys. As the polio vaccine is made with monkey kidney tissue, an alarming side effect has been the transmission of SV40 monkey virus to humans. During the 1940s and 50s, tissue from monkeys infected with SV40, was inadvertently used in vaccines. Studies of that period have shown an increase in various diseases, from breathing difficulties to leukaemia. Since 1961, polio vaccines have to be screened for SV40,[20] although recent reports suggest polio vaccines may still be contaminated with SV40.[21]

Variant CJD

A government investigation into 5 cases of vCJD near Southampton discovered that 2 of the 5 cases had received a polio vaccine (OPV) in 1994 taken from the same batch of vaccines. The report concluded that the risk of contracting vCJD from the polio vaccine was "incalculably small". However in October 2000, the brand of polio vaccine in question was withdrawn from use, "solely as a precaution", because the manufacturer's assurances had proved "inaccurate".[22]

Polio vaccines can be made using tissue from calf foetuses, and so they contain a theoretical risk of passing on BSE to children in the form of vCJD. Vaccine manufacturers are meant to comply to strict European guidelines that are in place to ensure that infected tissue is not used, and current OPV polio vaccines now only use bovine material sourced in Australia, New Zealand, Canada or USA.[23]

Why are we still vaccinating for polio?

The polio vaccine is still recommended because:

1. The risk of polio itself is much higher than the risk of the polio vaccine.
2. There is no wild polio in the Western world now, but there is still polio elsewhere in the world. For example, in 1990 China reported 5,065 cases, USSR reported 337 cases and India 7,340. With the ease of travel between most countries it is possible that polio could be brought in to the West.

1 Neustaedter. The Immunization Decision. North Atlantic Books, California. 1990.
2 Christina Head. An Educated Decision. The Lavender Hill Publishing Company. 1999
3 Neustaedter, op. cit.
4 Lynne McTaggart. The Vaccination Bible. What Doctors Don't Tell You. 1997.
5 National Statistics. Social Trends No 32: 2002 edition.
6 Figures from Statutory Notification of Infectious Diseases (NOIDS).
7 Joce et al, BMJ, 1992; 305:79-81.
8 Oostvogel et al, Lancet, 1994; 344: 665-70.
9 Mertens & Eggers, The Lancet, 1984, ii 1390.
10 Leon Chaitow. Vaccination - Dangers Delusions and Alternatives. C.W. Daniel. 1987.
11 Joce et al, BMJ, 1992, op. cit.
12 www.whale.to website - (Source: 20th century Mortality CD, Office of National Statistics.)
13 Trevor Gunn. Mass Immunisation: A Point in Question. Cutting Edge Publications. 1992.
14 Joce et al, BMJ, 1992, op. cit.
15 A new guide to childhood immunisations. Health Promotion England, and the NHS. 2001.
16 A new guide to childhood immunisations, op. cit.
17 www.misc-kids FAQs
18 Joce et al, BMJ, 1992, op. cit.
19 Manufacturers information sheet for a polio vaccine.
20 Viera Scheibner PhD. Vaccination. 1993.
21 The Informed Parent, Issue 4, 2002.
22 www.info.doh.gov.uk - from a Department of Health press release dated 17/12/2001.
23 www.info.doh.gov.uk - op. cit.

CHAPTER 14

MMR

A lot of press lately has concentrated on the controversy surrounding the MMR jab. We will look at each of the three diseases in turn, and their treatment and prevalence in the UK. We will then examine the options for vaccination, how effective the vaccines are, and look at the side effects of the vaccines.

MEASLES

Measles is one of the M's in MMR

What is measles?

Measles is a highly infectious viral disease, which tends to appear in epidemics every two to three years. It usually occurs in the spring, and mainly affects children. Measles is the most contagious disease that we know,[1] and is passed from child to child by coughs and sneezes. It is so contagious, that it could be caught by someone in a doctor's waiting room two hours after a child with measles had been there.

Eight to fifteen days after your child comes into contact with measles, her symptoms will be like those of a cold with a high fever. Small red spots with white centres (Koplik spots) may appear on the inside of her cheeks. Her temperature will fall for a day and then rise. A blotchy, slightly elevated pink rash will appear on the third to fifth day of measles. You'll first see the rash behind your child's ears, then on her face and then elsewhere. The rash lasts for three to five days. Your child is infectious throughout this period.

In most cases the symptoms soon subside but complete recovery may take two to four weeks. In a few cases the rash is accompanied by a severe bout of fever, and your child's eyes can be very irritated by the light. This indicates that complications have arisen (see below for complications).
The most likely age of contracting measles is from one to six years old and, if your child gets measles once, she will have immunity for life, and will not get measles again.

What is the treatment for measles?

You can treat mild forms of measles at home. If complications arise, your doctor will prescribe antibiotics or send your child to hospital if the complications are severe.

Are there any alternative treatments for measles?

Many studies have shown that Vitamin A supplements can reduce the risk of severe illness or death associated with measles.[2] A low level of Vitamin A in the body has been linked to increased illness and death.[3] [4] Children with the lowest levels of Vitamin A showed the worst symptoms during and after measles. They were more likely to develop eye symptoms, to have a fever above 40°C, to end up in hospital, and to die from measles.[5] This has been demonstrated in a small study of 180 children in Tanzania where there was a seven-fold reduction in children under two dying from measles following a Vitamin A supplementation programme.[6]

Vitamin A is found in lamb's liver, cod liver oil, carrots, kale, spinach, butter, dried apricots, broccoli, cheese (especially cheddar and parmesan), mango and eggs. An excess of Vitamin A is toxic, so if you're planning to use Vitamin A supplements, please consult a nutritionist. Pregnant women should not take Vitamin A supplements.

What are the dangers if my child catches measles?

You will see many different figures concerning the likelihood of complications from measles. Before we list those complications bear in mind two facts:

1. The Oxford Handbook of Clinical Specialties provides a whole list of measles side effects, and then states that you can expect "complete recovery in rich countries - but it [measles] is a serious mortal disease in poor countries." [7]
2. Many of the more serious cases of measles in the developed world are seen in children with weak immune systems.

Death

- The last child to die from acute measles in England and Wales, was a two-year-old child in 1992.[8]
- Between 1992 and 1999, there were 15 measles-related deaths in England and Wales. All but one of these were in older people.[9]
- In Ireland, there was an epidemic of measles in the year 2000. Of the 1,603 reported cases, three children died.[10]
- In the Netherlands in 1999/2000, there were 2,300 cases of measles. Three children died, and four developed encephalitis (inflammation of the brain). 53 went to hospital, and 500 were treated at home for measles complications.[11]
- Children who die from measles are more likely to be those with malnutrition or some other serious medical condition.
- More than one million children die each year worldwide from measles infection.[12] The vast majority of these are in Third World countries. In the Western world, measles is a "relatively mild disease".[13]
- You will see measles death rates ranging from 1 in 2,500 cases[14] up to 1 in 10,000.
- Death rates from measles are high in the under-one's, then lowest in the one to nine-year-olds, and then start to rise again.[15]

Severe complications

- Encephalitis. This is a dangerous swelling of the brain that could appear seven to ten days after the measles rash. Your child will be drowsy, and it will be difficult to keep her awake. She'll have a headache, and be disturbed by bright light, and she could become unconscious.[16] You should seek urgent medical attention. Encephalitis affects one in a thousand cases.[17] This figure is a worldwide figure and does not relate to well-nourished children in hygienic situations where the level of this complication is more likely to be 1 in 10,000 or 1 in 100,000.[18] Of those people that get encephalitis, 15% will die, and about one in five will suffer brain damage.
- SSPE. This is a fatal complication which can occur years after your child has had measles. SSPE occurs in one in a million cases of measles.[19]

Other complications

- Brain infection,
- Convulsions - 1 in 200 cases of measles lead to convulsions.[20]
- Blindness,
- Bacterial infection,
- Pneumonia,
- Bronchitis
- Ear infections - 1 in 20 cases,[21]
- Diarrhoea - 1 in 10 cases.

Many of the statistics available are taken from all measles cases including those in the Third World. The death rate is extremely low in healthy well-nourished children.

What are the chances of my child catching measles?

Measles is a highly contagious disease. There are currently around two or three thousand cases of measles in England and Wales each year, with 340 in London alone. That means approximately 1 in every 1,500 children under the age of four will catch measles. However the true amount maybe much less, because a high proportion of suspected measles cases do not turn out to be measles after all.[22] Indeed, two years ago, about 60% of the cases noted as measles, mumps, or rubella by local GPs were sent to the labs to confirm that the diagnosis was correct. Only 2% of the cases previously thought to be measles, were actually measles. The Government's Public Health Laboratory states: "Notification data on these infections are no longer a valid indication of the true incidence of the disease." [23] In other words, there are far fewer measles cases in reality, than actually reported in the official figures.

In America more than 90% of people who are not immune (i.e. not vaccinated) will get measles if they are exposed to the virus.[24]

By 1997/98, 91% of children under two had been given the MMR jab. However, in the light of the MMR controversy, this figure has now fallen to 88%,[25] and so more children are at risk from catching measles.

Table 14: Breakdown of measles cases in England & Wales, by age, for the year 2001.[26]

Age range	Number of cases
0 - 1 year	581
1 - 4 years	1,151
5 - 9	302
10 - 14	86
15 - 24	60
25 - 44	53
45 - 64	19
65+	9
Not known	25

1 Poland & Jacobson, Archives of Internal Medicine 1994; 154:1815.
2 Hussey & Klein, New England Journal of Medicine, 1990; 323:160-4.
3 Sommer et al, Lancet, 1986; 1:1169-73.
4 Sommer et al, American Journal of Clinical Nutrition, 1984; 40: 1090-1095.
5 American Journal of Diseases in Children 1996; 146:182-186.
6 Lynne McTaggart. The Vaccination Bible. What Doctors Don't Tell You. 1997.
7 Collier, Longmore & Hodgetts, Oxford Handbook of Clinical Specialties, OUP, 1997.
8 Public Health Laboratory Service - www.phls.org.uk - Facts & Figures. 23/01/2001.
9 Public Health Laboratory Service website, op. cit.
10 The website of the National Disease Surveillance Centre, Ireland - www.ndsc.ie
11 www.ndsc.ie, op. cit.
12 Kassianos, Immunization Childhood & Travellers Health, Blackwell Science, 2000.
13 GlaxoSmithKline website - Measles/Mumps/Rubella.
14 Kassianos, op. cit.
15 Salisbury & Begg, Immunisation against infectious disease, Dept. of Health, HMSO, 1996.
16 Charlish, Vaccination and Immunization. What Does Your Child Need? Thorsons, 1996.
17 Kassianos, op. cit.
18 Robert Mendelsohn, East West Journal, November 1984.
19 Lynne McTaggart, op. cit.
20 Kassianos, op. cit.
21 Kassianos, op. cit.
22 Statutory Notification of Infectious Diseases (NOIDS).
23 NOIDS Quarterly Report July to September 2000.
24 Website of the Centers for Disease Control and Prevention - www.cdc.gov - part of the US Department of Health and Human Services.
25 National Statistics. Social Trends No 32: 2002 edition.
26 Figures from Statutory Notification of Infectious Diseases (NOIDS).

CHAPTER 15

MUMPS

Mumps - the second M in MMR

What is mumps?

Mumps is a common viral infection that mainly affects school-aged children. The virus is spread in the air, and symptoms appear two to three weeks after your child is first exposed to mumps. It may start with a fever, a headache or vomiting, and then the mumps trademark: your child's salivary glands in his neck will swell. A gland on one side of his face often swells up before the other side, and sometimes only one side will be affected. The symptoms usually vanish in three days, but your child will remain infectious until the swelling completely disappears.

Complete recovery from mumps is the norm, and if your child has had mumps he will then have lifelong immunity from the disease.

What are the dangers if my child catches mumps?

The mumps infection may spread to other salivary glands, and also to the pancreas, to the brain (where it can cause aseptic meningitis) and to the testicles. It is not unusual to spread to the testicles, and is rarely serious except in adult men. In most cases, everything returns to normal within a week. It very rarely causes infertility because in the unlikely event of a testicle being affected and sterility resulting, the other testicle can still work effectively.[1]

Meningitis after natural mumps has been reported to occur at a rate of approximately 1 in 400 cases. Mumps is a common cause of viral meningitis in the under-15's.[2] Aseptic and viral meningitis are both usually mild, and run their course untreated.[3]

1 in 25 children with mumps will get some form of hearing impairment, although this is most often temporary.[4] In the US, before the mumps

vaccination was introduced, mumps was a major cause of deafness in children - it occurred in approximately 1 in 20,000 reported cases of mumps.[5]

Encephalitis (see previous chapter) is thought to occur once in every 200 mumps cases. Death from mumps is rare, and occurs for the most part in adult cases.[6]

What is the treatment for mumps?

Your doctor should be called to confirm that your child has mumps. He should then be kept at home for about ten days, but does not have to stay in bed. He'll feel like plenty of cool drinks and if you wrap a hot water bottle and rest it by his sore face, he'll find it soothing.

What is the risk of my child contracting mumps?

There are about two or three thousand cases of mumps each year in England and Wales.

Table 15: Breakdown of mumps cases in England & Wales, by age, for the year 2001.[7]

Age range	Number of cases
0 - 1 year	45
1 - 4 years	495
5 - 9	439
10 - 14	873
15 - 24	470
25 - 44	311
45 - 64	108
65+	30
Not known	31

A substantial proportion of these cases is shown subsequently not to be mumps.

As we said with measles, because of the current low uptake of the MMR jab, more children risk being exposed to mumps.

---

1 Robert Mendelsohn, East West Journal, November 1994.
2 Salisbury & Begg, Immunisation against infectious disease, Dept. of Health, HMSO, 1996.
3 www.eMedicine.com 23/5/2002.
4 Kassianos, Immunization Childhood & Travellers Health, Blackwell Science, 2000.
5 Website of the Centers for Disease Control and Prevention - www.cdc.gov - part of the US Department of Health and Human Services.
6 Neustaedter, The Immunization Decision. North Atlantic Books, California. 1990.
7 Figures from Statutory Notification of Infectious Diseases (NOIDS).

CHAPTER 16

RUBELLA

Rubella - the R in MMR

What is rubella?

Rubella is also known as German measles. It is a mild, highly contagious viral infection, which mainly affects children. Your child will contract rubella by close contact with another rubella sufferer.

Her first symptoms will appear two to three weeks after contracting the disease. She will have a headache, a sore throat and a slight fever. Her neck will swell and feel sore. A rash will appear and tiny pink spots will spread from her face and neck to the rest of her body. The spots will disappear within seven days, but your child will remain infectious for a further three to four days. Very rarely (about 1 in 6,000 cases), your child could suffer encephalitis (a swelling of the brain) as a result of rubella.[1]

If your child gets rubella, it usually means immunity from the disease for the rest of her life.

While rubella is generally a very mild disease in children, it can cause foetal abnormalities in up to 90% of babies born to mothers who are infected with rubella during the first three months of their pregnancy. These abnormalities are called the Congenital Rubella Syndrome (CRS) and include impaired vision and hearing, limb defects, mental retardation and heart malformations. Doctors recommend the rubella vaccination for all children to ensure they do not pass on rubella to their mothers or other women who may be pregnant.

What is the treatment for rubella?

No treatment is usually needed.

What is the risk of my child contracting rubella?

In 2001 in England and Wales, there were about 1,500 cases of rubella,[2] although minor epidemics of the disease tend to run in cycles of four to six years, when there can be around six thousand cases annually. Children tend to get rubella in the spring or summer. With fewer children currently having the MMR jab, there is more chance of catching rubella.

Table 16: Breakdown of rubella cases in England & Wales, by age, for the year 2001.[3]

Age range	Number of cases
0 - 1 year	402
1 - 4 years	661
5 - 9	228
10 - 14	69
15 - 24	59
25 - 44	67
45 - 64	11
65+	5
Not known	13

A substantial proportion of these cases is shown subsequently not to be rubella.

1 Charlish, Vaccination and Immunization. What Does Your Child Need? Thorsons, 1996.
2 Figures from Statutory Notification of Infectious Diseases (NOIDS).
3 NOIDS.

CHAPTER 17

MEASLES, MUMPS AND RUBELLA - THE IMMUNISATION OPTIONS

What are the options for protecting your child against measles, mumps and rubella?

1. Expose your child to the measles, mumps and rubella diseases, risking side effects, but giving him lifelong immunity.

2. Give your child the triple MMR vaccine at the recommended age of 12 to 15 months. This is the Government's desired option. See chapter 18.

3. Give your child three single vaccines, one for measles, one for mumps, one for rubella, spread out over a few weeks, at around 12 to 15 months. See chapter 20.

4. Wait until your child is older, say 24 months, before giving him the MMR injection.

What are the pros and cons of NOT vaccinating your child against measles, mumps or rubella?

The Pros:

- Your child may get each of the diseases naturally in a mild form, and then have lifelong immunity.

- Your child will not be exposed to any dangers from the vaccination.

- Your child may not get the diseases at all.

- If your child is exposed to measles, and you are concerned about the dangers of the disease, a measles vaccine should still protect your child if it is given within three days of a measles outbreak. This is not the case with mumps and rubella as your body takes longer to develop the antibodies to those diseases.[1]

The Cons:

- Your child may contract one of the diseases naturally and suffer serious complications, perhaps even death.
- Your daughter may not get rubella as a child, and so will have no immunity. Then as a pregnant woman, she would be at risk of contracting rubella, leading to a 90% chance of giving birth to a baby with foetal abnormalities. However, if your daughter has not had rubella by the time she reaches puberty, you can have her tested for rubella antibodies. If she has them, then she is immune; if not, she can have the single rubella vaccine (see below for more details) to protect her baby if she becomes pregnant.
- Your child may contract rubella, and pass it on to a pregnant woman.
- Your son may not contract mumps as a boy, and so would have a small risk of infertility if he contracted mumps as an adult. See chapter 15.

What are the pros and cons of the triple MMR jab?

The Pros:

- It provides protection against the childhood diseases of measles, mumps and rubella in 90% of children.
- Only one visit is needed to the doctor, so it's easier to ensure more people get immunised.

The Cons:

- There is a risk of side effects from the jab. See chapters 18 and 19.
- It is unclear how long immunity from the vaccine lasts. See chapter 18.

What are the pros and cons of the single vaccines?

The Pros:

- You will protect your child against each of measles, mumps and rubella.
- You avoid the MMR triple jab with its publicised risk of side effects.
- You let your child recover from one jab, before giving him the next.

The Cons:

- It is the measles virus that is linked to the controversy over MMR and autism. Both the triple MMR jab and the single measles vaccine contain the live measles virus.
- You are leaving your child unprotected against the diseases while he completes a course of single vaccines.[2]
- At the time of writing, the single vaccines have not been sanctioned by the British Government, and so are only available privately, often at a substantial cost. Because of the high demand, there is a risk that safety levels may be compromised by some clinics using unlicensed single vaccines.[3]
- The research of the MMR triple vaccine is much more up to date than research done on the single vaccines.

What are the pros and cons of giving your child the MMR jab when he is older?

The Pros:

- Your child will have a stronger immune system, and so his body should be better able to cope with any toxins in the MMR vaccine.

The Cons:

- Your child will be exposed to measles, mumps and rubella for longer.

---

1 Salisbury & Begg, Immunisation against infectious disease, Dept. of Health, HMSO, 1996.
2 Why is MMR vaccine preferable to single vaccines? Published in July 2002 by PHLS.
3 www.info.gov.uk/doh - Department of Health press release dated 14/11/2002.

CHAPTER 18

THE TRIPLE MMR JAB

How well does the MMR vaccine protect my child against measles, mumps and rubella?

The Government states that the MMR vaccine is 90% effective against measles and mumps, and 95% effective against rubella. A booster jab is needed to ensure that 95% of the population are immune. This will ensure that enough people will be immune to measles, so that the disease will be unable to cause epidemics and will die away.[1]

In 1995, 475 children who had been given the MMR triple jab were tested for resistance to each of the diseases. 99% were resistant to rubella, 69% were resistant to measles and 81% were resistant to mumps. The report recommended the booster jab to ensure the elimination of the disease.[2]

In the late 1980s there were anything from 50,000 to 100,000 cases of measles in the UK each year. MMR was introduced in 1988. By 2001 there were 2,286 measles cases. This tells us that the incidence of measles has reduced, if not wholly, then certainly partly due to the MMR jab. It also tells us that media reports about measles epidemics do nothing more than fuel the flames of the MMR controversy - there are measles outbreaks every year.

In the eighteen years before the MMR jab was introduced, there were an average of 13 deaths per year from measles in the UK. In the four years following the jab's introduction 11 people died in all.[3] No child younger than ten has died from measles since 1992, in England and Wales.

Before MMR was introduced, 1,200 people went to hospital each year with viral meningitis caused by mumps. Now, there are almost no cases.[4] Official records for the incidence of mumps only started in 1988, with the introduction of MMR, so figures comparing how may people had mumps before and after 1988 are estimates. The Government figures are shown in Table 17 below.

Table 17: The incidence of mumps in England & Wales, from 1985.[5]

Year	Number of mumps cases, per 100,000 people
1985	5.4
1986	5.4
1987	11.0
1988	2.5
1990 onwards	Less than 1

In other words, since MMR was introduced, less than 1 person in every 100,000 people gets mumps.

In the five years before MMR was introduced, there were about 43 cases a year of congenital rubella syndrome (children with birth defects due to their mothers catching rubella during pregnancy). Since the introduction of MMR, there are now less than two cases each year.[6]

How long does immunity last?

Resistance to measles, mumps and rubella has been shown to persist for over 11 years following the MMR jab.[7]

When should my child have the triple MMR jab?

12 to 15 months, by injection, and a booster before your child starts school, at around four years of age.

When should my child NOT have the triple MMR jab?

Doctors recommend not to vaccinate if your child:

- Has a severe allergy to eggs,
- Has an allergy to antibiotics,
- Has an immuno-suppressive illness, or there is a history of it in your family,

- Has an active infection, respiratory illness, or lymphomas of any kind,
- Has had a previous adverse reaction to the MMR vaccine,
- Is pregnant, or planning a pregnancy in the next three months,
- Is a breast-feeding mother.

Furthermore, alternative practitioners recommend not to vaccinate, if a child

- Has had a previous adverse reaction to any vaccine.

What's in the triple MMR jab?

The injection used now is called MMR II and contains live measles virus (Edmonston strain), live mumps virus (Jeryl Lynn B strain), live rubella virus (Wister RA 273 strain), neomycin sulphate (an antibiotic), human albumin, dipotassium hydrogen phosphate, disodium hydrogen phosphate, hydrolysed gelatin, medium 199 (a mixture of amino acids, mineral salts, vitamins and other components), monosodium glutamate, phenol red, potassium dihydrogen phosphate, sodium bicarbonate, sodium dihydrogen phosphate, sorbitol, and sucrose. The product contains no preservative.[8]

What are the side effects of the triple MMR jab?

This is the big area of controversy and media interest at the moment. Before we go any further it is worth stating that approximately one million doses of MMR are administered in the UK annually,[9] 600,000 of those to children under two.[10] Bear that figure in mind when considering how many people are suffering side effects from the jab. A second figure to remember is that no child under 10 in England and Wales has died from measles since 1992.

Having said that, as we mentioned in chapter 1, some scientists question what happens to the individual components of the jab when they are combined in the triple vaccine. Research has shown that more people react to combined jabs than to single vaccines, even when the single vaccine used was a stronger dose. For example, in one study, nearly 1 in every 3 children showed a measles rash when given a measles/mumps combined vaccine. Of the children who were given the measles vaccine on its own, only 1 in 30 developed a rash, even though the single vaccine was six times the strength of the measles part of the combined vaccine. Another study compared people given a measles and rubella combined jab with those people given the jabs alone. There were more cases of fever and diarrhoea in those people given the combined jab.[11]

MMR side effects according to the Government

The Department of Health's immunisation booklet states that the three different vaccines in the MMR jab may have different side effects at different times:

- "Six to ten days after their MMR vaccine, some children may become feverish, develop a measles-like rash and go off their food as the measles part of the vaccine starts to work.

- In the six weeks after the vaccine, your child may (very rarely) get a rash of small bruise-like spots. If you see spots like these, show them to your doctor." [12]

- About 1 in 100 children may get a mild form of mumps, about three weeks after their immunisation. A gland on the side of your child's face will swell.[13] This is one of the symptoms of mumps. " Your child will not be infectious and they can mix with other people as normal.

- About one child in every thousand who have the immunisation may have a fit, which is usually caused by a fever and is called a 'febrile convulsion'. But if a child has not been immunised and they get measles, they are ten times more likely to have a fit." [14]

- If your child has a fit six to eleven days after the jab, it is probably caused by the measles component of the triple vaccine.[15] You should seek your doctor's advice immediately.

- Although encephalitis (a dangerous swelling of the brain) has been reported in one in a million doses, the risk of a child getting encephalitis from measles is more common, although no-one agrees on exactly what that risk is. Some say that it is as much as one case of encephalitis in 1,000 cases of measles.[16] Others put the risk down at one case in 100,000.[17]

- The Government states that it is even less common to have side effects after the pre-school booster,[18] and when side effects do happen, they are usually milder. However some scientists fear that the booster jab could be the straw that breaks the camel's back: the final stress on your child's immune system after all the earlier vaccines she has had.[19]

MMR side effects according to the vaccine manufacturers

The patient information leaflet, provided in the vaccination packet by Aventis Pasteur MSD, warns that your child could suffer the following additional side effects:

- tiredness,
- sore throat,
- headache,
- nausea and vomiting,
- mild local reactions (where the needle enters the skin),
- swelling of neck glands,
- swelling of the testes (rarely),
- deafness (rarely).
- A blood clotting disorder which leads to spontaneous bruising and prolonged bleeding after injury. This occurs for 1 in every 30,000 doses in the UK and 1 in 40,000 in the US.
- Allergic reactions that lead to a swelling and redness at the injection site,
- anaphylactic shock,
- an itchy swollen rash,
- pain in the joints,
- arthritis (swelling and movement restriction of the joints). This is more likely in adult women and is rarely long term.
- Cough, runny eyes and nose,
- a moderate fever of 38.3ºC (101ºF) or a high fever above 39.4º C (103ºF) may occur, normally five to ten days after the jab.
- Inflammation of nerves in the eyes one to three weeks after the jab, causing headaches and visual disturbance (rare).

- Guillain Barré Syndrome, (weakness or numbness of the limbs, and usually with full recovery). This is very rare and it is not clear if this is caused by the injection or not.

Furthermore, Wellcome, one of the three original manufacturers of the MMR vaccine in Britain reported that, along with many of the side effects listed above, the vaccine also causes:

- SSPE (fatal but extremely rare), and
- measles which doesn't follow the usual symptoms. Atypical measles is an "especially vicious form of measles" that occurs in vaccinated children. It can be much more serious with more complications than measles itself.[20]

The Pasteur Merieux MSD insert ends by saying "Most people do not have any serious or long-lasting reactions to MMR II." [21]

Other possible side effects from the MMR jab

A study by the Public Health Laboratory Service found that for one in every 24,000 doses, the jab caused a rare non-fatal blood disorder known as IPT. IPT occurred in vaccinated children five times more than in non-vaccinated children. It is probably caused by the rubella component of the triple jab.[22]

A Danish follow-up study reports that 1 in 12,500 doses of the MMR vaccine has led to children staggering when walking. This is characteristic of ataxia, when the brain fails to control the limbs. Most cases were mild and short-lasting.[23]

Between July 1990 and April 1994, 5,799 adverse incidents following the MMR vaccine were reported to the US Vaccine Adverse Events Reporting System. These incidents included 3,063 cases requiring emergency medical treatment, 616 hospitalisations, 54 children left disabled, and 30 deaths. The US National Vaccine Information Center believes that because of massive under-reporting, these figures represent only 10 to 15% of the total number of side effects caused by the MMR vaccine.[24]

Parents have reported many side effects that have been unproven: [25]

- meningitis (see below),
- autism (see below),

- epilepsy,
- behavioural and learning problems,
- leukaemia,
- multiple sclerosis,
- cerebral palsy,
- death - 26 British families claim their children died after the MMR jab.

Meningitis
There used to be three different types of MMR vaccine available in the UK. However in 1992 two were withdrawn due to "reports of generally mild transient meningitis caused by the mumps vaccine virus". The jab currently in use - MMR II - contains the Jeryl Lynn mumps vaccine and has a much lower risk of meningitis.[26] A Finnish report, discussed in more detail below, looked at all MMR side effects over a 14-year period. In this time period, there were two cases of meningitis, both within seven days of an MMR jab. Three million children were given the jab, which contained the Jeryl Lynn mumps vaccine.[27] So the chances of getting meningitis following an MMR jab are 1 in 1½ million.

Any report that you read linking the MMR vaccine to meningitis is more likely to be taken from research made when the old Urabe strain of the mumps virus was still in use.

Diabetes
There has been a huge increase in the number of cases of juvenile diabetes in recent years. Many people believe this is linked to the increase in vaccinations given to our children. One side effect of both the mumps and rubella viruses is known to be diabetes, so researchers question whether the MMR jab itself could also lead to diabetes. Studies in Finland and Sweden both found no link between the MMR jab and diabetes;[28] whereas one study in New Zealand showed a 60% increase in diabetes cases following a mass hepatitis B immunisation campaign of six-week-old babies.[29] If there is a connection between MMR, or any vaccine, and diabetes, it appears to affect children with a disposition to auto-immune diseases - those are diseases where the body attacks itself. If you have any history of auto-immune diseases in your family, then talk through these issues with your doctor.

In the next chapter we will look at the controversy surrounding the possible link between MMR, autism and bowel disorders.

---

1 Salisbury & Begg, Immunisation against infectious disease, Dept. of Health, HMSO, 1996.
2 Miller et al, Vaccine, 1995; 13:799-802.
3 Salisbury & Begg, op. cit.
4 A new guide to childhood immunisations. Health Promotion England, and the NHS. 2001.
5 Salisbury & Begg, op. cit.
6 A new guide to childhood immunisations, op. cit.
7 Pasteur Merieux MSD Manufacturer's Insert, March 1996.
8 Pasteur Merieux MSD Manufacturer's Insert, op. cit.
9 Alexander Harris website - www.alexharris.co.uk.
10 Nicoll et al, BMJ, 1998; 316:715-716.
11 Wakefield & Montgomery, Adverse Drug Reaction Toxicol. Rev. 2000; 19(4): 284 - 292.
12 A new guide to childhood immunisations, op. cit.
13 Salisbury & Begg, op. cit.
14 A new guide to childhood immunisations, op. cit.
15 Farrington et al, The Lancet 1995; 345:567-9.
16 Kassianos, Immunization Childhood & Travellers Health, Blackwell Science, 2000.
17 Robert Mendelsohn, East West Journal, November 1984.
18 Salisbury & Begg, op. cit.
19 Wakefield & Montgomery, op. cit.
20 Viera Scheibner PhD. Vaccination. 1993.
21 Pasteur Merieux MSD Manufacturer's insert, op. cit.
22 Farrington et al, The Lancet op. cit.
23 Plesner AM et al, Acta Paediatrica 2000; 89(1):58-63.
24 Lynne McTaggart. The Vaccination Bible. What Doctors Don't Tell You. 1997.
25 Alexander Harris website, op.cit.
26 The Chief Medical Officer, 1992.
27 Peltola et al, Lancet 1998; 351 (9112)
28 Diabetes UK website - www.diabetes.org.uk, June 2000.
29 National Vaccine Information Center website - www.909shot.com

CHAPTER 19

MMR, AUTISM AND INFLAMMATORY BOWEL DISEASE

In 1998, Dr Andrew Wakefield[1] raised concerns that the MMR vaccine might increase the risk of autism after finding possible links between inflammatory bowel disease, autism and the MMR vaccine. Dr Wakefield analysed twelve children with previously normal development, who had recently become autistic or experienced some other neurological loss. They all had gut problems - normally diarrhoea and abdominal pain. The parents of eight of these children believe the problems began within two weeks of the MMR jab. Dr Wakefield called for further investigation. An editorial in the same issue of The Lancet expressed concerns about the validity of the study.

Since then, there have been many studies considering whether the MMR jab is linked to autism. At the time of writing this, no link has been proven, and none disproven, and research from both camps goes on. Dr Wakefield is of the opinion that parents know their own child best, and feels it would be wise to listen to those parents who believe that their children have been affected by the triple MMR jab.

So what exactly is autism?

- Autism is a severe psychiatric disorder of childhood starting before the age of two and a half.
- There is no cure.
- Boys are three to five times more likely to get it than girls.
- There is likely to be a genetic predisposition to autism.[2]
- Autistics have severe difficulties in communicating and forming relationships with other people.
- Behaviour problems and anxiety can sometimes be controlled with behaviour therapy and drugs. "A good teacher is more effective than a good doctor." [3]
- Autism covers a wide spectrum of disorders, from mild to severe, including Asperger's Syndrome - a form of abnormal personality where your child shows a lack of interest in other people, stilted and pedantic

speech, and an excessive preoccupation with a very specialised interest (such as timetables).

- Because of the confusion in diagnosis, it is hard to state how many people are autistic in the UK. One figure says that about 1 in a 100 are classified under the autistic spectrum disorder. Latest figures indicate that 1 in 86 primary school children are autistic.[4]

What is inflammatory bowel disease (IBD)?

IBD is an umbrella term for two specific illnesses - ulcerative colitis and Crohn's disease:

- With ulcerative colitis, your colon (large intestine) becomes inflamed and ulcerated. The symptoms are diarrhoea with blood and mucus, and stomach pains. It can be treated by drugs, steroids, bed rest and sometimes surgery.

- Crohn's disease mainly affects the small intestine. Symptoms are similar to ulcerative colitis, but with less bleeding, and more severe abdominal pains, and fever. Drugs aren't effective, but steroids, restriction of certain foods (cereals, yeast, dairy) and surgery can all improve, but not cure, the condition.

How are IBD and autism linked?

Studies from as early as 1961 have suggested that inflamed or dysfunctional intestines may lead to autism and other behavioural problems, so Dr Wakefield has discovered nothing new here. One theory suggests that the gut is not completely breaking down certain chemicals in the food we eat, and these left-over chemicals are indirectly affecting chemical patterns in the brain. This change in brain function leads to behavioural problems.[5]

What is the theory that links the MMR jab, autism and IBD?

The theory linking the MMR vaccine to autism and IBD is based on the evidence that the diseases themselves can lead to behavioural and gut problems. One of the small risks of your child getting measles is that he may develop encephalitis (swelling of the brain). This can lead to behavioural disorders. Rubella contracted during pregnancy is a known cause of autism.[6]

If the diseases can result in these problems, then, the theory goes, so can the live viruses in the vaccine. What's more, Wakefield believes that by combining the three viruses in one jab, you are exposing the child's immune system to a situation it wouldn't experience in nature, and problems could occur. Studies in the past have shown that if a child is exposed to measles, mumps and rubella in an unusual pattern (for instance, all three at the same time), then he could possibly develop autism.[7]

In a 1999 study, a team of scientists including Andrew Wakefield, sent questionnaires to 7,000 people born in 1970 in Britain. 37 had IBD, and 7 of them had had measles and mumps diseases in the same year. The researchers concluded that if your child was exposed to *both* measles and mumps in the same year (by natural illness, but by implication by the triple jab or single jabs), he would be more likely to suffer from gut problems. This conclusion was also supported by research in Iceland, which noted an increase in cases of IBD followed on from measles and mumps epidemics.[8]

However Wakefield and his colleagues also found that the timing of exposure to measles was important. If your child contracted only measles before he was two, then he would not be more likely to suffer from IBD.[9] And as a follow-up they showed that if your child has the single measles vaccine before the age of two, it would not lead to gut problems.[10] This is why Dr Wakefield supports the use of single licensed vaccines.

In a further study published in 2002, Dr Wakefield and his colleagues took samples from the guts of children with developmental disorders who also had bowel disease. They found that 75 out of 91 children had signs of a measles virus in their gut, compared with only 5 out of 70 healthy children.[11] The majority of the children examined had had the MMR vaccine. Some had had the single measles vaccine. This does not, however, *categorically prove* a link between the MMR triple vaccine and autism. It signals that more research is still needed.

What other evidence links MMR, autism and IBD?

- The MMR vaccine was introduced in 1988. At that time 1 in 2,200 children were diagnosed as autistic. As said earlier, the current rate of autism is 1 in 86 primary school children.[12]
- The Autism Research Unit has said a lot of factors could explain the increase in autism, but wouldn't rule out the MMR jab.[13]
- Because the onset of autism tends to occur before the age of two and a half, and the MMR jab is given between the ages of 12 and 15 months, the Government claims that any apparent links between the jab and autism are down to a coincidence of timing. One of the children seeing Dr Wakefield had the MMR jab at the age of 4 and then developed autism, a year and a half after the normal age of the onset of autism.[14]
- Some researchers question whether autism ever occurs in unvaccinated children, who weren't already suffering from another immune disease.[15]
- Before the MMR jab was introduced, trials were run to monitor the side effects on children. In one study, 12,000 children were monitored for 21 days; in another, children were monitored for 28 days. Anti-MMR campaigners claim that it is wholly inadequate to stop looking for side effects after only three to four weeks. They question whether that was long enough to find out whether any brain damage had occurred.[16]

What studies have disproved the link between autism, IBD and MMR?

Many scientists question Dr Wakefield's findings, claiming the samples were too small, or that he studied people sent to him because of their illness, and not people selected at random. There have been several studies, that look at the number of people with autism, the timing of the MMR jab, and reported side effects. Here are a few of the findings:

- One study considered children with autism born since 1979 in 8 North Thames health districts. It found a steady increase in cases of autism, with no sudden jump after the introduction of the MMR vaccine in 1988. Parents most often reported first noticing symptoms of autism at around the age of 18 months, after the MMR vaccine would have been received.

This was the case with vaccinated and unvaccinated children. The researchers conclude: "our analyses do not support a causal link between MMR vaccine and autism. If such an association occurs, it is so rare that it could not be identified in this large regional sample." [17]

- In February 2003, The Committee on Safety of Medicines in the UK reviewed studies involving 500 children with autism, and concluded that there was no link between MMR and autism. They found that the age of children when parents first became concerned about autism was the same, whether or not they had been given the MMR jab. Professor Alasdair Breckenridge who chaired the meeting said: "MMR is very effective at preventing serious and occasionally fatal diseases. Like all other effective medicines and vaccines, it has some associated adverse effects but these are far outweighed by its benefits." [18]

- Rates of autism in the United States began to increase long after the MMR jab was introduced in 1971.[19] A study in California looked at the increase in the number of children given the MMR jab from 1980 to 1994, and compared it with the increase in autism cases in the same period. Reported cases of autism in California rose by 373% in those 14 years, however there was only a 14% increase in the number of children given the MMR jab. The researchers conclude that the rise in autism is not linked to the MMR vaccine.[20]

- Dr Eric Fombonne, a psychiatrist from Maudesley Hospital in London has said that any apparent rise in cases was due to wider recognition by doctors of the symptoms of autism. He said rates of regressive autism, which has been linked to MMR, have not changed since before the vaccine was introduced.[21]

- A recent study looked at records of all the children born in Denmark from 1991 to 1998. Over half a million children were born in this period. 82% of them received the MMR vaccine. There were 738 cases of some form of autistic disorder amongst all the children. The study found that the vaccinated children were no more likely to get autism than the unvaccinated children. They also found that autism developed irrespective of when the child had had the jab.[22]

- A study in Sweden found no difference in the number of autism cases in children born before the introduction of the MMR vaccine and children born after it.[23]

- In Finland, every adverse event reported to doctors following the introduction of MMR in 1982 has been analysed. Researchers have followed up those children reporting gastrointestinal symptoms (GI) after receiving the MMR vaccine. Approximately three million children received the MMR jab in Finland between 1982 and 1996. 31 children suffered GI symptoms, and all recovered - normally within a week. None showed any lasting effects. No child developed an autistic disorder, although the researchers were not actively looking for this. There were two cases of meningitis reported within seven days of vaccination.[24]

- An American study looked at 155 people with inflammatory bowel disease, and found that their vaccination history had no bearing on whether or not they got IBD. They concluded that the MMR or other vaccines containing the measles virus did not increase the risk of IBD. In fact, children given MMR after 18 months of age, appeared to have less risk of getting IBD, than those not vaccinated at all.[25]

Conclusions

There have been two types of studies carried out to link MMR, autism and IBD. The first type looks at the statistics: for example, when autism began to rise, compared with when MMR was introduced. As with all political issues, there is always more than one way to interpret figures, so the jury is still out on that one.

The other type of study is trying to replicate Andrew Wakefield's findings to see if any measles virus lingers in the guts of people with autism and/or inflammatory bowel disease. If Wakefield's results are repeated, the next question is to work out whether that measles virus came from the disease or the vaccination. Research is currently ongoing in this area.

So as things stand at the moment:

- Hundreds of millions of people worldwide have received measles-containing vaccines without developing bowel disease or behavioural problems.[26]

- At the time of writing, the parents of over 1,000 children have been given legal aid to pursue legal action against four vaccine manufacturers. They claim their children have suffered damage as a result of the MMR triple vaccine. In the majority of cases, this damage has led to autism and IBD, but there are also cases of encephalitis and epilepsy. The court case is due to start in April 2004.[27]

- Whilst no link has been proven, and none disproven, that the MMR vaccine can lead to autism, there are parents and scientists who remain convinced that their children's autism was a direct result of the vaccine.

---

1 Wakefield et al, Lancet, 1998; 351(9103):637-41
2 Halsey & Hyman, Pediatrics 2001; 107(5):E84.
3 Collier, Longmore & Hodgetts, Oxford Handbook of Clinical Specialties, OUP, 1997.
4 The Saturday Telegraph Magazine, 8th June 2002.
5 Wakefield et al, Lancet, op. cit.
6 Halsey & Hyman, Pediatrics op. cit.
7 Wakefield & Montgomery, Adverse Drug Reaction Toxicol. Rev. 2000; 19(4): 284 - 292.
8 Ekbom, Gastroenterology, 1999; 116:988-990.
9 Ekbom, Gastroenterology, op. cit.
10 Morris et al, American Journal of Gastroenterology, 2000; 95(12):3507-12.
11 Uhlmann et al, Molecular Pathology, 2002; 55 (2): 84-90.
12 The Saturday Telegraph Magazine, 8th June 2002.
13 BBC News Website.
14 Wakefield et al, Lancet, 1998; op. cit..
15 Scheibner & Hancock, www.vaccine-info.com, February 2001.
16 Miller et al, Practitioner, 1989; 233:69-73.
17 Taylor et al, Lancet, 1999; 353(9169):2026-9.
18 www.nhs.uk - the NHS website - press release dated 15/2/03, entitled "No scientific evidence linking autism and MMR."
19 Halsey & Hyman, Pediatrics 2001, op. cit.
20 Dales et al, Journal of the American Medical Association, 2001; 285 (9); 1183-5.
21 BBC News Website.
22 Madsen et al, New England Journal of Medicine, 2002; 347:1477-1482.
23 Gillberg and Heijbel, Autism, 1998; 2:423-424.
24 Peltola et al, Lancet 1998; 351 (9112).
25 Davis et al, Archive of Pediatric and Adolescent Medicine, 2001; 155(3):354-9.
26 Chen & Stefano, The Lancet 1998; 351: 611-12.
27 Alexander Harris website www.alexharris.co.uk, and personal communication.

CHAPTER 20

THE SINGLE VACCINES OF MEASLES, MUMPS AND RUBELLA

If you are unsure about the triple MMR jab, then you could give your child the single vaccinations. Your child would need six single jabs: the three primary doses of measles, mumps and rubella, followed later by the pre-school boosters for each of the three diseases, if you want to give these. You can space out the primary vaccines over a period of, say, three months, to give your child six weeks to recover between each jab. The Government does not advise the single vaccine option. It says you are leaving your child open to the risk of catching the disease while he is waiting for his course of jabs to be completed. It also feels that fewer children would complete a course of six vaccines, compared to a course of two MMR jabs (the initial dose, and the pre-school booster).[1]

At the time of writing this, the single vaccines are not available on the NHS. There are clinics that will give you the single vaccines, but you will have to pay, and it can be expensive. It is still legal for any GP to give your child the single jabs, but they are unlikely to, because they are constrained by the Department of Health's policy to recommend the combined MMR jab. If the surgery has high levels of MMR vaccine uptake in its area, it is entitled to money bonuses.

There is also the risk that single vaccines may be brought into the UK illegally to fulfill the recent demand. You need to make sure your doctor is using a licensed and approved vaccine, and that it is stored correctly. The Government advises that if you do try and get single vaccines, you ask: [2]

- exactly which vaccine your child is being offered;
- when and where the vaccine was tested;
- what the result of those tests were, in terms of the vaccine's safety, its strength and its purity;
- what post-vaccination follow-up of your child is offered by the clinic carrying out the jabs.

If you want to find out where to get a single vaccine near you, look at www.jabs.org.uk.

THE SINGLE VACCINE FOR MEASLES

How effective is the vaccine?

The single measles vaccine has been shown to be 96% effective[3] which means that at least four in every 100 children given the jab may still catch measles.

A study in America in 1985 looked at an outbreak of measles at two schools in Texas. The researchers looked at 1,806 secondary school students, 99% of whom had been vaccinated against measles. The students were tested for their immunity levels and over 95% of them were immune to measles. There were 74 students for whom the vaccination did not appear to work. 14 of them contracted measles. In spite of almost total vaccination coverage, measles can still occur.[4]

In the UK, since the 1940s and until the single jab was introduced, there was anything from 160,000 up to 800,000 cases of measles per year, with peaks every two years. The single measles vaccine was introduced in 1968. The number of measles cases had declined to 50,000 to 100,000 cases by the late 1980s, when MMR was introduced.[5] So the single measles jab may have been responsible for reducing measles disease, but these figures prove it is not totally effective.

In November 1994, the Government launched a massive immunisation campaign in the UK to prevent a measles epidemic. 8 million children aged 5 to 16 were given a double measles and rubella vaccine. Studies then showed that, following this jab, children were 85% less likely to catch measles.[6]

Deaths in the UK from measles had been in steady decline before the single measles vaccine was introduced. See Table 18 below. One plausible explanation for this decline was better nutrition and improved living conditions.

Table 18: Number of deaths from measles in England & Wales from 1901 - 1999.[7]

Year	Average number of deaths from measles per year
1901 - 1910	10,548
1911 - 1920	9,894
1921 - 1930	4,240
1931 - 1940	2,035
1941 - 1950	504
1951 - 1960	128
1961 - 1970* *Single Measles vaccine introduced in 1968	85
1971 - 1979	21
1980 - 1989* MMR vaccine introduced in 1988	13
1990 - 1999	2

How long will my child be protected against measles?

Immunity from the measles vaccine wears off anything from 11 to 15 years after the jab,[8] leaving a pregnant woman open to the disease. Measles during pregnancy may result in low birth-weight infants, miscarriage, premature labour and possible foetal abnormalities.[9]

When should my child have the measles jab?

12 to 15 months, and then a pre-school booster.

When should my child NOT have the measles jab?

Doctors recommend not to vaccinate if your child:

- Has a severe allergy to eggs,

- Has an allergy to antibiotics,
- Has an immuno-suppressive illness, or there is a history of it in your family,
- Has an active infection, respiratory illness, or lymphomas of any kind,
- Has had a previous adverse reaction to the MMR vaccine,
- Is pregnant, or planning a pregnancy in the next three months,
- Is a breast-feeding mother.

Furthermore, alternative practitioners recommend not to vaccinate, if a child

- Has had a previous adverse reaction to any vaccine.

What's in the measles jab?

The single measles jab contains live measles virus cultured in chick embryo tissue culture. It can be produced using neomycin, sorbitol and hydrolized gelatin.[10]

What are the side effects of the measles jab?

When talking about the single measles vaccine, we must remember that it is the measles virus itself that researchers believe is involved in the unproven link between the triple MMR jab and the autism cases. Both the triple MMR jab and the single measles jab contain the live measles virus. It is possible, therefore, though as yet unproven, that the single vaccine could also lead to autism.

Having said that, in one study Andrew Wakefield and his colleagues, found no link between the single measles vaccination and inflammatory bowel disease. They found an increased risk of inflammatory bowel disease if the measles vaccine was given after the age of two, but the numbers involved were so small that they called for further studies.[11] As mentioned earlier Wakefield's team also found there was an increase in gut problems if patients had had measles and mumps in the same year.[12] Again, the numbers involved were small. This does not necessarily mean that if you give your child the single measles and mumps vaccines he will have gut problems.

One study has traced 3,545 people who received a single live measles vaccination in 1964 during the testing period for the vaccine. None of this group contracted measles. 14 of them had Crohn's Disease, and 11 of them suffered from ulcerative colitis. The researchers compared this group with a control group of 11,000 people who had not been vaccinated against measles. They found that the measles vaccination led to a 300% increased risk of developing Crohn's Disease and a 250% increased risk of ulcerative colitis.[13]

Another study found that there was one serious reaction for every 5,000 doses of the measles jab. These included anaphylactic shock, convulsions and neurological disorders.[14]

In the mass immunisation campaign of November 1994, when eight million children were given measles and rubella vaccines, there were 560 serious reactions and three reported cases of thrombocytopenia, which is a disorder of the blood. That's about one serious reaction for every 14,000 doses of the measles/rubella jab.[15]

Following the same campaign, there were three cases of Guillain Barré syndrome (a nerve disease leading to weakness in the limbs, and usually with full recovery). Normally, in the same timescale, there are between one and eight cases.[16] In other words your child is very unlikely to suffer from Guillain Barré syndrome, but if he does, he is just as likely to get it randomly, as to get it from a measles jab.

A study over a four-week period in America in the 1960s calculated that there were 1½ cases of encephalitis for every one million doses of measles vaccine. Over any random four-week period there were normally 2.8 cases of encephalitis for every 1 million children.[17] So not only is encephalitis as a side effect of the measles vaccine very rare, in many cases where the measles jab has been blamed, statistics imply that the encephalitis may well have happened by chance all the same.

As mentioned earlier, there is a new type of measles, atypical measles that only occurs in vaccinated children and is much more serious with more complications.[18]

In Guinea-Bissau children who had caught measles were found to have less allergies than children who had been vaccinated against measles.[19]

Are there any other dangers from the measles jab?

A mother, if she has already had measles, will give her baby a natural resistance to the disease for the first six to twelve months of the baby's life. However if the mother was vaccinated and never had measles, then the baby will not inherit that natural resistance. Studies have looked at the natural measles immunity level of six-month-old babies of mothers vaccinated against measles. 93% of these babies had no immunity.[20] Therefore the more we vaccinate people, the more likely it is that their babies under the age of one, will contract measles. It is in this age group, that the disease is most dangerous.[21] In the USA, the proportion of measles cases in under-six-month-olds has risen from around 1% of all measles cases in 1985 to over 5% in 1992.[22]

In America there were 27,672 measles cases in 1990. A quarter of these cases were in the under-15-month-olds (that is before they were vaccinated). This led to a higher death rate in America from measles, of 3.2 deaths per 1,000 measles cases compared to one death per 1,000 cases normally.[23] The American government has lowered the routine age for measles vaccination from 15 months to 12 months to overcome the loss of natural immunity to measles in babies.[24]

THE SINGLE VACCINE FOR MUMPS

How effective is the single mumps vaccine?

The single mumps vaccine has never been part of the immunisation programme in the UK, as the mumps vaccine was first introduced as part of the MMR triple jab in 1988. However a mumps vaccine was licensed in the USA in 1967 and put to widespread use from 1977. There were 100,000 mumps cases per year in the 1970s in America. This fell to between 3,000 and 5,000 cases in the early 1980s, although in 1987, mumps incidence rose to 13,000 cases.[25]

The mumps vaccine has been rated as 75 to 95% effective,[26] and mumps immunity lasts at least 15 years.[27] Homoeopaths question why we are vaccinating against mumps, since, if the vaccination is thought to wear off, then children are more likely to contract mumps when they are older, and it is likely to be more serious.[28] Infertility from mumps is only a problem in adolescent and adult men, but even then it is rare.

When should my child have the single mumps jab?

12 to 15 months and then a pre-school booster.

When should my child NOT have the mumps jab?

Doctors recommend not to vaccinate if your child:

- Has a severe allergy to eggs,
- Has an allergy to antibiotics,
- Has an immuno-suppressive illness, or there is a history of it in your family,
- Has an active infection, respiratory illness, or lymphomas of any kind,
- Has had a previous adverse reaction to the MMR vaccine,
- Is pregnant, or planning a pregnancy in the next three months,
- Is a breast-feeding mother.

Furthermore, alternative practitioners recommend not to vaccinate, if a child

- Has had a previous adverse reaction to any vaccine.

What's in the single mumps jab?

Live attenuated Jeryl Lynn strain of the mumps virus grown either in chick embryo tissue culture, or sometimes in tissues containing human diploid cells. It can be produced using neomycin, sorbitol and hydrolyzed gelatin.[29]

What are the side effects of the single mumps jab?

- A burning sensation at the injection site.
- A mild fever.
- Rarely children may get a mild form of mumps, about three weeks after their immunisation. A gland on the side of your child's face will swell.[30] This is one of the symptoms of mumps. Your child will not be infectious and can mix with other people as normal.
- Fits, encephalitis, deafness and other nervous system reactions have occurred very rarely, although no causal link has been established.[31]
- We have already said that the mumps part of the MMR vaccine has been linked to aseptic or viral meningitis, which are usually mild forms of meningitis. The single vaccine has also been linked with encephalitis and epilepsy. However all this research was made when the old Urabe strain of the mumps virus was still in use. In 1992 a vaccination with the Jeryl Lynn strain of the mumps virus replaced the other vaccines. Evidence suggests it is safer.
- As discussed in chapter 18, some researchers believe that juvenile diabetes is a side effect of the mumps and rubella viruses, and so the mumps vaccine itself could also lead to cases of diabetes.[32]

THE SINGLE VACCINE FOR RUBELLA (GERMAN MEASLES)

As we mentioned earlier, if you decide against vaccination when your child is a toddler, you can wait until your daughter reaches puberty to have her tested for rubella antibodies. If she has these antibodies, it means she would have had rubella already without you realising it, and therefore has natural immunity for life. If she doesn't have the antibodies, she can have a single rubella vaccine. She may have to go private, because the government has now discontinued the rubella vaccine for 10 to 14-year-old girls, preferring to give rubella immunisation to young children.

How effective is the single rubella vaccine?

The single rubella vaccine was introduced in the UK in 1970 to protect pregnant women. It was given to pre-pubescent girls and women without natural rubella resistance. Before 1970, about 85 to 90% of women had natural immunity to rubella, which they would have acquired by having German measles as a child. By 1987, 97 to 98% of women had immunity to rubella, so the single vaccine had been pretty effective in protecting most women against rubella.[33]

In 1972 there were 750 terminations in pregnancy because of rubella. In 1987, there were 164 cases of rubella in pregnant women.[34]

In November 1994, eight million children were given a measles and rubella double vaccine to avoid a possible epidemic. Table 19, below, shows that rubella cases have started to drop from 1997. This is thought to be when the results from the 1994 campaign kicked in.

Table 19: Number of reported cases of rubella in England & Wales, 1991 - 2001.[35]

Year	Number of cases
1991	7,174
1992	6,212
1993	9,724
1994	6,326
1995	6,196
1996	9,081
1997	3,260
1998	3,208
1999	1,954
2000	1,653
2001	1,515

Research has shown that some children will still have immunity eleven years after being given the rubella vaccine.[36] However children react differently to the jab, and some show no evidence of rubella immunity when tested four to five years after the rubella vaccination.[37] So, if your daughter has the rubella vaccine, she should be protected against rubella while she is young, but the immunity from the jab could run out when she is older. She could therefore contract rubella in pregnancy, resulting in possible damage to her unborn child. This has happened in the past. A woman in Germany, who had been vaccinated three times against rubella, gave birth to a boy with CRS (Congenital Rubella Syndrome). He was born deformed, because his mother had had rubella during the first three months of her pregnancy.[38]

When should my child have the rubella jab?

The Government recommends rubella as part of MMR at 12 to 15 months and a pre-school booster.

When should my child NOT have the rubella jab?

Doctors recommend not to vaccinate if your child:

- Has an allergy to antibiotics,
- Has an immuno-suppressive illness, or there is a history of it in your family,
- Has an active infection, respiratory illness, or lymphomas of any kind,
- Has had a previous adverse reaction to the MMR vaccine,
- Is pregnant, or planning a pregnancy in the next three months,
- Is a breast-feeding mother.

Furthermore, alternative practitioners recommend not to vaccinate, if a child

- Has had a previous adverse reaction to any vaccine.

What's in the rubella jab?

Live rubella virus, neomycin sulphate and human foetal tissue. The killed vaccine also contains lactose, sorbitol, dextran 10 and amino acid.[39]

What are the side effects of the rubella jab?

The disadvantage of having the single rubella vaccine at puberty is that the side effects are more common at this age. This may be because a 15-month-old can't report their symptoms.

The most common side effect of the rubella vaccine is joint pain and arthritis. This is also a complication of the rubella disease itself, and can last for up to two years. About 3% of children who have the jab will suffer temporary arthritis, and about one in five adult women[40] given the rubella vaccine can get chronic arthritis lasting for at least a year.[41] The Vaccine Injury Compensation Programme in America, and the US Court of Federal Claims have accepted a link between the rubella vaccine and the onset of arthropathy (a disorder of the joints).[42] In the 1994 Measles Appeal, the Department of Health admitted to doctors that 11% of first time recipients of the rubella vaccine will suffer temporary arthritis.[43]

Another side effect is chronic fatigue syndrome, which can affect adult women given the rubella vaccine.[44]

As we have mentioned there is evidence that juvenile diabetes is a side effect of both the mumps and the rubella viruses. Therefore the rubella vaccine itself could be a cause of juvenile diabetes.[45]

---

1 Why is MMR vaccine preferable to single vaccines? Published in July 2002 by PHLS.
2 Why is MMR vaccine preferable to single vaccines? op. cit.
3 Poland & Jacobson, Archives of Internal Medicine 1994; 154:1815.
4 Gustafson et al, New England Journal of Medicine, 1987; 316:771-774.
5 Salisbury & Begg, Immunisation against infectious disease, Dept. of Health, HMSO, 1996.
6 Salisbury & Begg, op. cit.
7 www.whale.to website & Public Health Laboratory Service website - www.phls.org.uk - Facts & Figures, 23/01/2001.
8 http://www.faqs.org/faqs/misc-kids/vaccinations/part2/ 23 January 2003.
9 Poland & Jacobson, op. cit.
10 www.whale.to/vaccines/ingredients.
11 Morris et al, American Journal of Gastroenterology, 2000; 95(12): 3507-12.
12 Ekbom, Gastroenterology, 1999; 116:988-990.
13 Thompson et al, The Lancet 1995; 345: 1071-1074.
14 Pollock & Morris, The Lancet 1983; 1: 753-757
15 Salisbury & Begg, op. cit.
16 Salisbury & Begg, op. cit.
17 Salisbury & Begg, op. cit.
18 Viera Scheibner PhD. Vaccination. 1993.
19 Shaheen et al, The Lancet 1996; 347: 1792-6.
20 Mulholland, The Lancet 1995; 345: 305 - 307.
21 Paediatric Infectious Disease Journal 1992 vol 11:525-9.
22 Centre for Disease Control & Prevention, Atlanta, Georgia, USA.
23 Poland & Jacobson, op. cit.
24 Dennehy, Clinical Microbiology Reviews 2001; 14: 872-908.
25 Neustaedter, The Immunization Decision. North Atlantic Books, California. 1990.
26 Neustaedter, op. cit.

27 Mumpsvax MSD manufacturers insert.
28 Lynne McTaggart. The Vaccination Bible. What Doctors Don't Tell You. 1997.
29 www.whale.to/vaccines/ingredients
30 Salisbury & Begg, op. cit.
31 Mumpsvax MSD manufacturers insert.
32 National Vaccine Information Center website - www.909shot.com
33 Salisbury & Begg, op. cit.
34 Salisbury & Begg, op. cit.
35 All figures from Statutory Notification of Infectious Diseases (NOIDS).
36 Horstmann DM et al, Review of Infectious Disease 1985; 7 Suppl 1:S80-85.
37 Horstmann DM, Annals of Internal Medicine 1975; 83(3) 412-417.
38 Braun C et al, ACTA Paediatrica 1994; 83(6): 674-7.
39 Karpasea-Jones. Everything there is to know about vaccination. Vaccine Information Service. 2002.
40 Charlish, Vaccination and Immunization. What Does Your Child Need? Thorsons 1996.
41 Geier DA & Geier MA, Clin Exp Rheumatol 2002; 20(6): 767 - 771.
42 Weibel RE & Benor DE, Arthritis Rheum 1996; 39(9):1529-34.
43 Lynne McTaggart, op. cit.
44 Allen AD, Med Hypotheses 1988; 27(3):217-20.
45 National Vaccine Information Center website - www.909shot.com

CHAPTER 21

WHAT DO OTHER COUNTRIES DO ABOUT IMMUNISATION?

Most Western countries have very similar vaccination policies to the UK. However, there are some differences as well as some variation in infant mortality rates. We will look at the United States, Japan and Sweden.

Sweden and Japan have very good infant mortality rates. In the year 2000, both countries registered three infant (under-one-year-old) deaths for every thousand live births. This compares with five deaths per thousand in the UK, Holland, Germany, Canada and Australia. The USA has an infant mortality rate of seven per thousand live births.[1] There are many factors affecting a country's infant mortality rate, but alternative practitioners believe vaccination schedules could have a role to play.

United States

The population of America is 283 million. Its infant mortality rate is 7 per 1,000 babies. For children under five the mortality rate is 8 per 1,000 children.

In America the vaccination programme is compulsory and your child is not allowed to go to school without having had all the vaccinations. There is now a new compulsory vaccination against chickenpox and in some states Hepatitis B is also compulsory.

Table 20: Recommended Immunisation Programme in the United States:[2]

What is given	When it is given
Hep B	3 times: birth to 2 months, 4 months and 6 to 18 months
Hib	4 times at 2, 4, 6 and 12 to 15 months
Pneumococcal meningitis	4 times at 2, 4, 6 and 12 to 15 months
DTaP	5 times at 2, 4, 6 and 15 months and 4 to 6 years
IPV - polio	4 times at 2, 4 and 6 to 18 months and 4 to 6 years
Hep A	Twice: 24 months and 18 years
MMR	Twice: 12 to 15 months and 4 to 6 years
Varicella (chickenpox)	Once: 12 to 18 months
Td (Diphtheria and tetanus booster)	11 to 12 years

The meningitis C vaccine has not been recommended in America for three reasons:

1. There is a low risk of actually getting meningococcal disease.

2. There is no vaccine available against the Group B bacteria, which accounts for nearly half of the cases in America.

3. The meningitis Group C vaccine does not illicit an immune response in children under two.[3] In other words, the Americans do not think the meningitis C vaccine works for the under-two's.

However, because of the increased risk of college students contracting a meningococcal disease, the Advisory Committee on Immunization Practices has recommended that the vaccine be made available to students if they want it.[4]

The Americans do not administer DTaP with Hib for the first three doses, as there is evidence that the Hib part of the combined vaccine does not work in the under-one's.[5] In the UK, the alternative to DTaP is used for the under-one's. This alternative, namely DTP, is combined with Hib, to make the conjugate DTP-Hib vaccine given at 2, 3 and 4 months.

American Facts & Figures:

- In 2001, 13,573 side effects to the jabs were reported.[6]
- Disease levels in America have been in steady decline over the last century, and as in the UK, this decline started before the introduction of the vaccination programme.
- Measles peaked in 1941 with 894,134 cases. There were 13,000 cases in 1980, 27,000 in 1990, and now there are about 100 cases of measles a year.
- Mumps peaked in 1968 with 150,000 cases, and in 1999 there were less than 400 cases.
- Rubella incidence was at a high in 1969 with 57,000 cases annually. Now there are less than 300. In the 1960s there were about 20,000 cases each year of Congenital Rubella Syndrome (seen in babies whose mothers caught rubella when they were pregnant). This has now fallen to just 9 cases annually.
- Whooping cough peaked in 1934 with 265,000 cases. Disease levels fell to 1,700 cases in 1980, but have since risen to more than 4,000 in 1990, and 6,000 in 2000.
- Hib meningitis levels were running at about 20,000 cases per year before 1989. That has now dropped to 267 cases in 1999.
- Diphtheria, tetanus and polio are all now at negligible levels.[7 8]

Despite its rigorous approach to vaccinations, the US Government recognises that, as with all medicines, a small minority of people will be affected by vaccinations. The Government and US drug companies set up the National Vaccine Injury Compensation Programme in 1986. It has paid out more than $1 billion to families of children damaged by vaccines.[9] In the UK, parents can claim up to £100,000 if their children have been seriously vaccine-damaged.

Sweden

Sweden has a population of 8.8 million. Its infant mortality rate is 3 deaths per 1,000 infants. For children under five, the mortality rate is 4 deaths per 1,000.

Table 21: Immunisation schedule in Sweden:[10]

What is given	When it is given
DTaP	3, 5 and 12 months
Hib	3, 5 and 12 months
Polio (IPV)	3, 5, 12 months and 6 years
MMR	18 months and 12 years
Td (tetanus/diphtheria booster)	10 years
BCG	6 months

Sweden has a very high take-up rate for the third jab in the series of DTaP, Hib, and polio.

As mentioned in chapter 11, the whole cell pertussis vaccine was withdrawn in 1979 when its safety was widely questioned. There was a pertussis epidemic in the early 1980s. In January 1996, the new acellular (aP) vaccine was introduced, and take up levels are high again. There were 2,700 whooping cough cases in 2000, down from 10,000 in 1995.

There are no cases of diphtheria and polio in Sweden

Sweden has a very low infant mortality rate. This could be due to several factors, for example, it has a very high level of healthcare provision. However, Swedish children receive fewer jabs than British children, they are older when they are vaccinated, and they are given DTaP, instead of DTP. These factors could all have a bearing on infant mortality rates.

Japan

Japan has a population of 127 million. Its infant mortality rate is 3 deaths per 1,000 infants. For children under five, the mortality rate is 5 deaths per 1,000.

Table 22: Immunisation schedule in Japan:[11]

What is given	When it is given
DTaP	4 times from 3 months to 7 years
DT	11 to 12 years.
Polio	Twice from 3 months to 7 years
Measles	Once at 12 months
Rubella	Once at 12 months, or at 12 years
Japanese Encephalitis	Three times at 6 months to 7 years, 9 to 12 years and 14 to 15 years.
BCG	Three times at 0 to 4 years, 8 and 12 years

In 1975, Japan delayed the point that children were first vaccinated until they were at least two years old. Japan then zoomed from seventeenth place to first place with the world's lowest infant mortality rate.[12] In 1995 the immunisation schedule was changed. Typically a Japanese infant will now have twelve shots before their first birthday,[13] compared to 18 in the UK. Japan still has a very low infant mortality rate.

Japan does not use the MMR triple jab. This is because of the link to vaccine-related meningitis of the strain of MMR jab that was in use in Japan. The Japanese have withdrawn the jab, and as they do not have an alternative licensed triple vaccine, they administer the single vaccines of measles and rubella. They do not administer mumps.[14] As mentioned earlier, the UK used three types of triple jab up to 1992, and because of the link to meningitis, two of them were withdrawn.[15]

Take-up of the vaccination programme is generally very high.

Japanese Facts & Figures

- There were 515 reported adverse reactions to the vaccination programme in 2001 in Japan.
- There have been only two reported cases of diphtheria in the last two years, and no neonatal tetanus, although there were 90 cases of tetanus in 2001.

- Whooping cough was on the decline with as few as 42 cases in 1998, but in 2000 and 2001 there have been 3,700 cases each year.

- Measles was also on the decline with 899 cases in 1998. In the last two years, there have been over 22,000 cases of measles each year.[16] 21 people died from measles in 2001 - 11 of whom were under 18.[17]

- In 1970 to 1974, Japan began administering DTP to its children aged three to five months. The compensation system paid claims for 57 permanent severe reactions and 37 deaths in those four years. From 1975 to 1980, the DTP programme was not started until children were two. In those five years there were eight severe reactions and three deaths. By delaying DTP, there was a 90% reduction in severe reactions and deaths. In 1981 Japan introduced the acellular pertussis vaccine. In 1994 the primary course of DTaP was given to children "upon recommendation" from the age of 3 to 12 months.[18]

---

1 WHO website - country profile, WHO.int.
2 Centers for Disease Control & Prevention. 2001. Recommended childhood immunization schedule - United States 2001, & WHO website, op. cit.
3 Dennehy, Clinical Microbiology Reviews 2001; 14:872-908.
4 Dennehy, op. cit.
5 Dennehy, op. cit.
6 WHO website, op. cit.
7 WHO website, op. cit.
8 Dennehy, op. cit.
9 Article in The Times, October 2002.
10 WHO website, op. cit.
11 WHO website, op. cit.
12 LA Times, March 1st, 1990.
13 Japan Immunisation Schedule, http://idsc.nih.go.jp/yosuko99.
14 WHO website, op. cit.
15 Aventis Pasteur MSD website.
16 WHO website, op. cit.
17 The Informed Parent, Issue 4, 2002.
18 Infectious Agents Surveillance Report, Japan website http://idsc.nih.go.jp

APPENDIX 1

SOME FACTS & FIGURES

When reading a book like this, it seems that death from a childhood disease is far more likely than the reality. In this appendix, we'll break down some of the figures, so that you'll see we are talking in small numbers. And, it's worth remembering that driving a car, or crossing the road is far more dangerous than any childhood disease or vaccination. There are about 3,000 fatalities on Britain's roads each year - to put things in perspective. We're unsure whether or not that's any comfort.

Some population facts: [1]

- The population in the UK taken from the 2001 census is nearly 59 million.
- There are 660,000 children under 1.
- There are 2.8 million children aged between 1 and 4.
- You have a 1 in 14 million chance of winning the National Lottery, and a 1 in 55,000 chance of matching 5 of the 6 numbers.
- You have a 1 in 20,000 chance of being killed on the roads this year.

Childhood deaths

- 4,079 babies aged under-one died in the UK in 1998.[2] It is the most vulnerable time of life. However infant mortality has improved massively over the last century:
- In 1921, 84 of every 1,000 under-one-year-olds died.
- In 1951 this had come down to 50 children for every 1,000.
- In 2000, the figure stands at 5.6 children for every 1,000. In other words, for every 178 babies born in the UK each year, one child will die before it reaches its first birthday.
- The improvement in infant mortality in the last 80 years is "due to nutrition, hygiene and sanitation, better ante- and post-natal care, the immunisation programme, better medical techniques for premature babies, and the fall in the number of cot deaths." [3]

- 810 children aged one to four died in 1998 in the UK. That is one child dying out of every 3,649 one to four-year-olds.[4]
- The mortality rate in one to four-year-olds has also improved. In 1991, as many as 1,148 children died.

Some causes of death

Table 23: This chart shows some causes of death, ***across the whole population,*** *in England & Wales, in 1998.*[5]

Cause of death	Number of deaths, from all age groups
Whooping cough	4
Measles	3
Menigococcal infection	210
Meningitis	216
Sudden Infant Death Syndrome (cot death)	236
Motor vehicles	2,946

The three measles deaths in 1998 were in older people.[6]

1 www.statistics.gov.uk/census2001
2 Annual Abstract of Statistics 2000 edition. The number of under-1's who died in England & Wales in 1998 was 3,625.
3 National Statistics. Social Trends 2002 Edition No. 32.
4 Annual Abstract of Statistics 2000 edition. The number of one to four-year-olds who died in England & Wales in 1998 was 722.
5 Annual Abstract of Statistics 2000 edition.
6 Public Health Laboratory Service website - www.phls.org.uk - 23/01/2001.

APPENDIX 2

THE VACCINATION ALTERNATIVES - YOUR COURSE OF ACTION

As you will have gathered by now, there are alternatives to giving your child the vaccinations. The way we see it, you have the following options:

Your options:

1. Give your child the vaccination.

2. Give your child the vaccination, and then counter any side effects of the vaccination by giving him homoeopathic remedies.

3. Use an alternative approach to vaccination, either with homoeopathy, or another complementary approach.

4. Do not vaccinate, try and ensure your child has a healthy lifestyle, and hope he does not get the disease.

5. Let your child catch the disease, and so give him natural immunity for life.

Bear in mind, that you can decide on a different option for each childhood illness. You may, for example, decide that polio is too dangerous a disease to take a risk with, and so have your child vaccinated against it. On the other hand, you may feel that measles, mumps and rubella are less dangerous, and you may not like to risk the side effects of the triple MMR jab. In which case, you would choose a different course of action for those three illnesses.

So, having decided on your option for each disease, these are the appropriate courses of action you need to take:

1. Give your child the vaccinations:

Go and see your doctor. Your surgery will normally send out a reminder when your child is due for jabs.

2. Give your child the vaccination, and then counter any side effects by giving homoeopathic remedies:

You should visit a homoeopath before your child goes for his jabs. Your homoeopath will give you a remedy made from the vaccine itself. This can be given before and after the medical jab to reduce the severity of any side effects. A homoeopath will be able to advise you what to take, and when to take it.

3. Use an alternative approach to vaccination, either with homoeopathy, or another complementary approach.

A homoeopath will give you 'nosodes'. These are homeopathic remedies made from the disease itself, which strengthen the areas of the body that the particular disease targets. The idea behind this is that should your child contract a childhood disease, the nosodes ensure that he will not get it so severely.

4. Do not vaccinate, and hope your child does not get the disease.

If you decide not to vaccinate then it is wise to make sure that your child is as healthy as possible. You should try and get him to eat healthily (most of the time!) with plenty of fruit and vegetables and as little sugar as possible. Make sure that he is taking plenty of exercise and spends as much time as possible outside in the fresh air. Reduce his intake of toxins (such as antibiotics and vaccinations), and you can also use stimulatory therapies such as acupuncture, homoeopathy, osteopathy, herbalism and naturopathy.[1]

5. Give your child natural immunity.

To protect your child naturally, he will need to contract the disease. Many practitioners believe this will strengthen his immune system. In which case, do not vaccinate your child, and then make an effort to track down children with the disease.

The Contact Network has been established that will inform you if there is a common childhood illness in your area. There are also a growing number of parents giving measles parties. Finally the National Childbirth Trust in your area may be able to advise you if a common illness comes to town.

Contact Network
Lesley Dove
Phone: 020 8861 1233
Email: Lesley@vegan4life.org.uk

National Childbirth Trust
Alexandra House
Oldham Terrace
London
W3 6NH
Call for your nearest group: 0870 444 8707
www.nct-online.org

---

1 Trevor Gunn. Mass Immunisation: A Point in Question. Cutting Edge Publications. 1992.

APPENDIX 3

CONTACTS AND SUGGESTED READING

Books & Leaflets

A new guide to childhood immunisations, NHS, 2001.

MMR, The Facts, NHS, 2001.

Immunisations against Infectious Disease, Department of Health, HMSO 1996 (2003 edition out soon).

Scheibner Viera PhD, Vaccination, 1993.

Head, Christina. An Educated Decision. Lavender Hill Publishing Company. 1995.

Curtis, Susan. Homoeopathic Alternatives to Immunisation. Winter Press. 2002

Lynne McTaggart. Vaccination Bible. What Doctors Don't Tell You. 1997.

Gunn, Trevor. Mass Immunisation: A Point in Question. Cutting Edge Publications. 1992

Vaccination Groups

The Informed Parent Newsletter
PO Box 870
Harrow
Middlesex
HA3 7UW
Tel 020 8861 1022.

Vaccination Awareness Network
PO Box 6261
Derby
DE1 9QN
0870 444 0894
www.vaccine-info.com

JABS - the support group for vaccine-damaged children
1 Gawsworth Road
Golborne
Warrington WA3 3RF
01942 713 565
www.jabs.org.uk

What Doctors Don't Tell You
Satellite House
2 Salisbury Road
London SW19 4EZ
020 8944 9555
www.wddty.co.uk

Other Websites
www.immunisation.org.uk - the NHS website.
www.whale.to
www.thinktwice.com
www.vaccination.co.uk
www.apmsd.com - the vaccine manufacturer Aventis Pasteur MSD

Other Contacts
To find a homoeopath near you, contact:
The Society of Homoeopaths
4a Artizan Road
Northampton NN1 4HU
www.homeopathy-soh.org
01604 621400